RANGERS

THE **OFFICIAL** ILLUSTRATED HISTORY

First published in 2012
by HACHETTE SCOTLAND, an imprint of Hachette UK

1

Cataloguing in Publication Data is available from the British Library

Hardback ISBN 978 0 7553 19206

Typeset in Bosis and designed by Melvin Creative, Glasgow

Printed in Great Britain by
Butler Tanner & Dennis Ltd, Frome and London.

HACHETTE SCOTLAND
An Hachette UK Company
338 Euston Road
London NW1 3BH

www.hachette.co.uk

RANGERS

THE OFFICIAL ILLUSTRATED HISTORY

LINDSAY HERRON

INCLUDES **RARE** AND **EXCLUSIVE** PHOTOGRAPHY

Contents

Foreword by Sandy Jardine

Chapter	1	Road to Recovery	09
Chapter	2	Early Days	19
Chapter	3	Scottish League	35
Chapter	4	Scottish Cup	63
Chapter	5	League Cup	85
Chapter	6	Europe	105
Chapter	7	Ibrox	127
Chapter	8	Old Firm	149
Chapter	9	Managers	167
Chapter	10	Heroes and Legends	199
Chapter	11	Behind the Scenes	219
Chapter	12	The Fans	243

FOREWORD
Sandy Jardine

THE HISTORY of Rangers is rich and glorious, from the very inception of the club in 1872, through the remarkable feats and achievements of great players and great managers backed by an incredibly loyal and passionate support.

It is therefore entirely appropriate to reflect the great successes, the key figures and the times of adversity with the club's expansive photographic archive.

Rangers hold the world record for national championships won, clinching their 54th title in May 2011 when the curtain came down on Walter Smith's fantastic second spell as manager.

They have claimed the Scottish Cup 33 times and their record of 27 victories in the League Cup is equally impressive.

I am extremely proud to be a member of the team that lifted the European Cup Winners' Cup on May 24, 1972 in Barcelona's Nou Camp Stadium when Moscow Dynamo were defeated 3-2.

I also played in the 1967 Final when Rangers lost narrowly to Bayern Munich, and the club has appeared in two other finals – the inaugural Cup Winners' Cup of 1960/61 and the UEFA Cup Final of 2008.

Indeed, only Real Madrid, Barcelona, Sporting Lisbon and Anderlecht have played in more European matches than Rangers, with the first involvement coming back in 1956.

From humble beginnings Rangers became the giants of the game, firstly under manager William Wilton and then the incomparable Bill Struth, from the turn of the 19th century through to the outbreak of the Second World War.

Some of the most legendary figures in the club's history come from these early days and they are thoroughly represented in the Rangers Hall of Fame which I am also honoured to have been involved with since its inception in 1999.

Men like Davie Meiklejohn, Alan Morton, Bob McPhail, Dougie Gray and Sandy Archibald are absolute giants in terms of their achievements.

Post-war, the famous Iron Curtain defence developed – Bobby Brown, George Young, Jock Shaw, Ian McColl, Willie Woodburn and Sammy Cox – and they were complemented by the flair of Willie Waddell and Willie Thornton.

For many Rangers supporters the team of the early 1960s was something special – Ritchie, Shearer, Caldow, Greig, McKinnon, Baxter, Henderson, McMillan, Millar, Brand and Wilson.

However, the Treble-winning teams of the 1970s – largely made up of the Cup Winners' Cup side – would certainly be on a par.

There is little doubt that the Graeme Souness and Walter Smith eras produced an incredible litany of success which included nine successive championships. Indeed it might well be the greatest period in the club's history.

We have had our dark days, of course, and none more horrific than the Ibrox Disaster on January 2, 1971 which claimed the lives of 66 supporters.
The pain and suffering of insolvency in 2012 was also an incredible strain on everyone connected with Rangers and it is a period we will never forget. There were those who revelled in our distress but the recovery process has already begun.

As you will learn from this excellent collection of photographs, Rangers has a history to be proud of and one that will continue for decades to come.

The great Bill Struth put it succinctly when he said: 'To be a Ranger is to sense the sacred trust of upholding all that such a name means in this shrine of football. They must be true in their conception of what the Ibrox tradition seeks from them. No true Ranger has ever failed in the tradition set him.

Our very success, gained you will agree by skill, will draw more people than ever to see it. And that will benefit many more clubs than Rangers. Let the others come after us. We welcome the chase. It is healthy for all of us. We will never hide from it.

Never fear, inevitably we shall have our years of failure, and when they arrive, we must reveal tolerance and sanity. No matter the days of anxiety that come our way, we shall emerge stronger because of the trials to be overcome.

That has been the philosophy of the Rangers since the days of the gallant pioneers.'

Charles Green and the Sevco consortium completed a deal for Rangers in May 2012.

Chapter 1
Road to Recovery

Peterhead, August 11, 2012,
Carlos Bocanegra leads out Rangers

"WE DON'T DO WALKING AWAY"

ALLY McCOIST

The **remarkable** Rangers spirit has never been more prevalent than in 2012 when a great institution endured the horror, pain and suffering of insolvency to emerge battered and bruised but with fresh hope, its pride and integrity intact and ready for a journey of recovery.

The successful takeover by the Sevco consortium, headed by Charles Green in May 2012, effectively rescued the club from potential oblivion, but there was a rash of punitive sanctions and punishments imposed by the Scottish football authorities for breaching a number of rules during the tenure of Craig Whyte.

At the end of it all, Rangers found themselves in Division Three, banned from signing players for a year, bereft of the majority of their major players who walked out for free – and that barely scratches the surface of the most remarkable story in Scottish football history.

Rangers were forced into administration on February 14, 2012 because Whyte had not paid any of the PAYE or VAT to HMRC, resulting in a £9million debt which was exacerbated by the existing legal battle over the use of Employment Benefit Trusts, with HMRC claiming around £50 million in back taxes with penalties and interest.

Administrators Duff & Phelps forged an agreement with the players to take wage cuts ranging from 75 per cent to 25 per cent in order to slash the monthly outgoings and keep the club going.

Rangers Fans Fighting Fund, raising over £600,000, and they supported the team in their droves – even selling out a legends match against AC Milan Glorie.

Good friends Linfield staged a match against Rangers in Belfast, handing over the profits to the Light Blues, and huge money-raising events were staged like the 1872 Walk around Ibrox involving Walter Smith, Nacho Novo and Mark Hateley among others.

The uncertainty was unbearable at times as various groups looked to

The SPL clubs voted against transferring the share of the 'oldco' to the 'newco' and Rangers were booted out of the top flight. They applied to join the SFL who were under pressure from the SFA and SPL to replace Rangers in Divison One. The SFA and SPL predicted massive financial problems for the Scottish game if this did not happen, but the SFL clubs opted to place Rangers in Divison Three.

The SFA then demanded the acceptance of a list of sanctions, including a 12-month signing embargo, before granting them membership of the Association and this deal was not completed until less than 48 hours before their opening match.

However, Rangers reappeared on the pitch at Glebe Park, Brechin in the first round of the Ramsdens Cup on July 29, and then eased into action in the Third Division with new players like Ian Black, Dean Shiels and Francisco Sandaza in their ranks.

SFL President Jim Ballantyne, Chief Executive David Longmuir and Vice President Ewen Cameron at the meeting when Rangers were admitted into Division Three of the League.

However, in adversity Rangers found a hero in the shape of manager Ally McCoist who worked for free for a period and coined the phrase 'we don't do walking away' in an impromptu TV interview at the beginning of the administration period – this became the mantra for the fans, who rallied magnificently. They ploughed money into the

take over the club but it was Sevco, headed by Charles Green, who completed the transaction on the last day of the 2011/12 season.

They tried to exit administration through a Company Voluntary Agreement which would have resulted in a small return for creditors, but main creditors HMRC blocked this and a 'newco' was formed.

The supporters flocked back too, queuing for hours to send season ticket sales soaring through the 36,000 barrier and set a European record for attendance with 49,118 for a fourth tier match in their opening home league match against East Stirlingshire. It will take time, but the recovery has started.

Joint Administrators David Whitehouse and Paul Clark from Duff & Phelps.

The Rangers supporters were galvanised during administration.

The backing of the fans was incredible and they sold out a Legends match at Ibrox between a host of former Ibrox stars and the AC Milan Glorie side led by Franco Baresi.

Passion was high among the fans and one of the money-raising ideas was the launch of red and black scarves (shown below by Lee McCulloch) which were snapped up in their thousands.

Franco Baresi and Walter Smith with host Jim White at a gala dinner ahead of the AC Milan Legends match at Ibrox.

Walter Smith and Sandy Jardine were heavily involved in Rangers Fans Fighting Fund events like the 1872 Walk around Ibrox.

There was an incredible show of strength by the Rangers supporters at the first match after administration was announced on February 14 against Kilmarnock, and their backing was consistently loyal through the painful and hurtful process.

Charles Green flanked by Sandy Jardine and Head of Football Administration Andrew Dickson at Perth on May 13, 2012, the day he concluded the deal to buy Rangers.

Nacho Novo and Mark Hateley joined Walter Smith on the 1872 Walk around Ibrox.

The board – Brian Stockbridge, Malcolm Murray, Imran Ahmad and Charles Green.

Ally McCoist was a tower of strength during administration.

Ian Black signs his deal with Charles Green.

Francisco Sandaza and Emilson Cribari were key signings.

Kevin Kyle shows the colours after joining Rangers.

Dean Shiels was a superb summer capture.

Chapter 2
Early Days

The first ever Rangers team shot from 1877

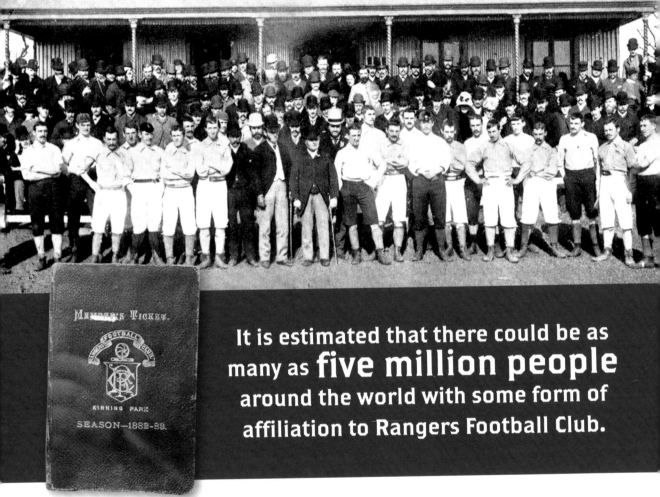

This shot is from September 8, 1888 at the first Ibrox Park when a Canadian representative team played Rangers during a tour of the UK. The match finished 1–1 with Robert Hotson scoring for Rangers. The teams that day were: Rangers: McAllister, A. McFarlane, D. Gow, R. Hotson, J. McIntyre, J. Muir, Thomas Wyllie, James Sloan, A.H. McKenzie, J. Gow, Eagleshaw. Canadians: Garrett, Brubacher, Killer, Pirie, Tom Gibson, Gordon, Bowman, Alex Gibson, Thomson, Webster, Krantz.

It is estimated that there could be as many as **five million people** around the world with some form of affiliation to Rangers Football Club.

It is therefore extraordinary to think that this Scottish institution with a name that resonates globally began in a carefree moment in the spring of 1872 when 16-year-old Moses McNeil, his brother Peter and good friends Peter Campbell and William McBeath struck upon the idea of forming a football team when walking in a park in Glasgow's West End.

Moses liked the name 'Rangers' having seen it in an English rugby annual, and the newly-formed team played their first ever match at Flesher's Haugh on Glasgow Green in May of that year against a team called Callander.

McNeil lived to the grand old age of 82 and was able to witness the incredible rise of Rangers from their humble beginnings to the imperious power and influence they held over the Scottish game in the 1920s and 1930s when they dominated relentlessly and set attendance records that will never be surpassed.

Rangers were nomadic in their early days, playing at Burnbank, Kinning Park and then the first Ibrox, the site of which is adjacent to the current Ibrox which became the team's home in 1899.

While McNeil is etched in history as the founder, there seems little

the first Championship, albeit not outright as they shared the honour with Dumbarton.

After 20 years of trying, they won the Scottish Cup for the first time in 1894, by which point William Wilton, then match secretary, was a pivotal figure in the development and organisation of the club.

Wilton became the club's first manager in 1899 and was hugely influential in setting the standards on and off the field that Rangers have maintained to this day.

result of the incredible success he achieved – 18 league championships, 10 Scottish Cups and two League Cups as well as a host of other domestic trophies, including all of the wartime Southern League titles.

Rangers were the kings of the game in the 1920s and 1930s with some of the greatest players in the club's history – men like Davie Meiklejohn, Alan Morton, Sandy Archibald, Andy Cunningham, Bob McPhail, Dougie Gray, Jimmy Smith and George Brown.

Moses McNeil.

Peter McNeil.

Tom Vallance.

doubt that Tom Vallance, who joined the young Rangers in 1873, was the most significant figure in the formative years in his role as captain and then as president, showing great leadership.

Rangers embraced the advent of professionalism and were founder members of the Scottish Football League in 1890 and promptly won

He was followed by the incomparable Bill Struth, who had been the trainer at the club before becoming boss in 1920 following the tragic death of Wilton in a boating accident on the Clyde.

Struth's reign was utterly astonishing not just for the fact that it lasted 34 years but as a

It was arguably the greatest period in the club's history as they won the title 14 times in 19 seasons up to the suspension of competitive play due to the outbreak of the Second World War.

FIRST TEAM TO WIN THE SCOTTISH CUP, 1893-1894.

J. Taylor (*Trainer*).
Back Row—H. M'Creadie, J. Steel, N. Smith, D. Haddow, D. Mitchell.
Sitting—A M'Creadie, D. Boyd, W. Wilton (*Secretary*), J. Drummond, J. MacPherson, J. Barker.
Front Row—R. Marshall, J. Gray.
Scottish Cup.   Glasgow Cup.   *See page 70.*

After 20 years of trying, Rangers finally won the Scottish Cup for the first time in 1894
when they beat Celtic 3-1 at Hampden in front of 17,000 with Hugh McCreadie, John Barker
and John McPherson scoring the goals on an historic day.

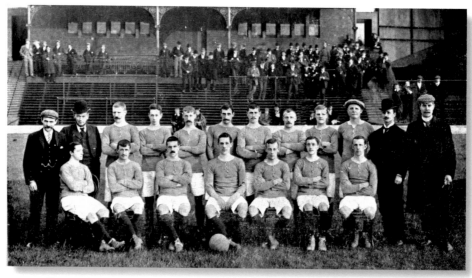

The astonishing feat of the 'Invincibles' in season 1898/99 is something that has scarcely
been emulated in world football. Rangers won all 18 of their league fixtures for a 100 per cent
record and only Ferencavaros of Hungary and Nacional of Uruguay have achieved something
similar. Our historic picture shows – Back (from left) James Wilson (trainer), James Henderson
(chairman), Nicol Smith, Davie Crawford, Neilly Gibson, Matt Dickie, James Stark, Bobby Neill,
Jacky Robertson, Jock Drummond, William Wilton (manager), A. MacKenzie (linesman).
Front – Johnny Campbell, John Graham, John McPherson, Robert Hamilton (captain), Findlay
Speedie, Andrew Sharp, Alex Smith.

THE THREE-CUP TEAM, 1896-1897.

J. Muir (*Committee*).
Standing—T Low, M. Dickie, N. Smith, J. Miller, T. Hyslop, A. Smith, J. Oswald, R G Neil.
Sitting—J. MacPherson, N. Gibson, D. Mitchell, A. M'Creadie, T. Turnbull.
Inset—J. Drummond.

Glasgow Cup.   Scottish Cup.   Glasgow Charity Cup.   *See page 96.*

Rangers' second success in the Scottish Cup came in 1897 when they hammered Dumbarton 5–1.
It was a memorable season as they won three trophies for the first time, collecting the Glasgow Cup
and the Glasgow Charity Cup as these two pictures show.

23

The Rangers' directors and officials look resplendent in their three-piece suits and ties as they pose with the Scottish Cup and Glasgow Cup in 1894. Tom Vallance is on the far left with William Wilton, front second right. Below are rare season tickets from the pioneering days which take pride of place in the Ibrox Trophy Room.

Original Members' Tickets

Duncan Graham spent two years as Rangers' chairman from 1932 to 1934 when the Bill Struth team was at the peak of its powers.

In the immediate post-Second World War years, William Rogers Simpson held the office of chairman at Ibrox.

Jimmy Bowie was a highly successful Rangers player and then served as chairman from 1934 to 1947, but was ousted when he suggested that Bill Struth be replaced as manager!

Joseph Buchanan was the Rangers chairman when the club broke their Scottish Cup hoodoo in 1928, ending a 25-year wait for the trophy.

Team
OF 1907

Rangers' first manager William Wilton set the standards for the club in the early days. This shot is from the 1907/08 season when Rangers went to Rothesay to prepare for the Glasgow Cup final against Celtic. Our researcher Neil Stobie has identified Alex Craig in the back row far right. The rest of the line-up is – Middle – Jimmy Wilson (trainer), Jimmy Gordon, John May, James Galt, David Taylor, William Wilton (manager). Front – John Dickie, R.C. Hamilton, George Livingstone, R.G. Campbell (captain), Alex Newbigging, Alex Smith, John MacDonald. Despite exhaustive research we cannot identify the other two people on the back row.

This is a medal from Rangers' first trophy success in 1879 when they defeated Vale of Leven 2–1 in the Glasgow Charity Cup final.

GLASGOW RANGERS F.C. Season 1911-1912.

1911–12 team group.

After winning the Double in 1934, Rangers embarked on a post-season tour of Germany and played five matches in 14 days against a German League Select side, winning four and losing one. This shot shows the squad with their hosts at King Frederick's Palace in Potsdam, near Berlin.

The 1926–27 squad: (back row, l-r) J. Purdon, W. Hodge, J. Smith, J. Osborne, W. Moyies, J. Hamilton, J. McGregor, R. Manderson, Jimmy Fleming; (middle row, l-r) W. Chalmers, Tom Hamilton, Sandy Archibald, Tully Craig, R. Ireland, D. Kirkwood, Jock Shaw, Geordie Henderson, Andy Cunningham; (front row, l-r) Bill Struth (manager) Davie Meiklejohn, Dougie Gray, Alan Morton, Arthur Dixon, Tommy Cairns, Tommy Muirhead, James Marshall, J. Gillespie (trainer).

Torry Gillick

One of the most exciting players of his era, Torry Gillick's Rangers career straddled the Second World War. Thus he was part of two great Ibrox sides, interrupted by a spell at Everton which made him the only player that Bill Struth signed twice.

Rangers embarked on a highly successful post-season tour to the United States in 1928 after their historic League and Cup double. They played ten matches, winning seven and drawing three, in which Bob McPhail scored 14 times. This is the side that beat the American League 6–0 in Brooklyn on June 23, 1928.
Back: James Bowie (director), Duncan Graham (chairman), Davie Meiklejohn (captain), Jock Buchanan, Tom Hamilton, Andy Cunningham, Tommy Muirhead, Bill Struth (manager). Front – Bob McPhail, Dougie Gray, Willie McCandless, James 'Doc' Marshall, Sandy Archibald, Tully Craig.

Jimmy Gordon (second left) was one of a number of Rangers players who saw active service in defence of their country. He served with the Highland Light Infantry in 1916. Gordon won five titles, three before and two after the Great War.

J. Dawson.   W. A. Cheyne.   T. Hart.   T. Brownlie.   T. McKillop.   R. Main.   G. Jenkins.
R. McDonald.   W. Hay.   J. Simpson.   J. Kennedy.   J. Smith.   J. Drysdale.   R. McPhail.   J. McHarg.   S. Roberts.
(Manager). A. Venters.   A. Winning.   G. Brown.   A. MacAulay.   D. Meiklejohn (Captain).   D. Kinnear.   T. Gillick.   J. Fiddy.   D. Gray.   A. Dixon (Trainer).

WINNERS OF
SCOTTISH CUP, SCOTTISH LEAGUE CHAMPIONSHIP AND SCOTTISH ALLIANCE CHAMPIONSHIP

1934–35 team group.

This is the league medal won by Bob McPhail for season 1929/30. Remarkably he won the title nine times during an incredible period of dominance for the Light Blues.

Having dominated the War years, Rangers won the 1946/47 Championship and the inaugural League Cup when official competition resumed. This picture shows (back, from left) – Sammy Cox, Charlie Watkins, Bobby Brown, George Young, Scot Symon and Jock Shaw. Front – Willie Waddell, Torry Gillick, Willie Thornton, Jimmy Duncanson and Jimmy Caskie.

31

Willie Woodburn is greeted by Glasgow's Lord Provost Sir Hector McNeil, flanked by Rangers team mates Willie Thornton and Willie Waddell, before Scotland faced France in a friendly which they won 2–0. Unusually Scotland wore the Lord Roseberry colours of primrose and amber hoops which was the change kit at the time!

No club has supplied more players to the Scottish national team than Rangers.

Jimmy Simpson and Jimmy Smith (front 1st and 2nd left) and Jerry Dawson (back 2nd right) report for duty.

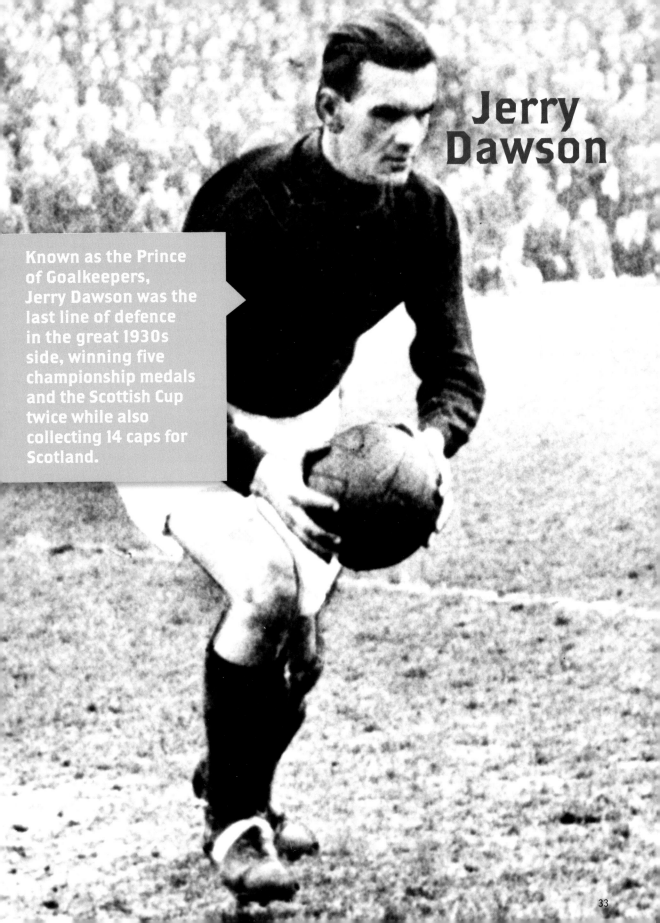

Jerry Dawson

Known as the Prince of Goalkeepers, Jerry Dawson was the last line of defence in the great 1930s side, winning five championship medals and the Scottish Cup twice while also collecting 14 caps for Scotland.

Sam English

The story of Ulsterman Sam English is one of the saddest in football and yet he remains an iconic Rangers figure as his league goals total of 44 in 1931/32 remains a club record and may never be beaten. It was in that first season – on September 5, 1931 – that he was fatefully involved in an accidental collision which subsequently claimed the life of Celtic goalkeeper John Thomson. Jimmy Fleming had crossed the ball from the right and English was preparing to shoot when Thomson dived at the striker's feet and smashed his head on English's knee. English was completely blameless. Later that night Thomson died of a fractured skull. English was haunted by the incident and also taunted unfairly by rival fans. He left Rangers after just two seasons.

Chapter 3
Scottish League

2011 Ibrox Dressing Room

BELL'S PREMIER DIVISION
WINNERS SEASON 96/97

THERE is **no other club** in world football that has dominated a domestic championship in the way that Rangers have ruled the roost in Scotland, with **54 titles** to their name since the inception of league football in 1890.

In 116 campaigns up until 2011/12 Rangers have also finished runners-up 30 times and they have only finished outside of the top three 14 times, which is another indication of the club's remarkable consistency over a prolonged period.

Rangers share the record with Celtic of winning nine successive league championships, achieving the terrific feat between 1988/89 to 1996/97 under the stewardship of firstly Graeme Souness and then Walter Smith.

The Light Blues shared the first ever championship with Dumbarton in 1891 when the two sides finished level on points. They could not be separated following a play-off match which finished 2–2, played at Cathkin Park in Glasgow.

They first won the title in their own right in 1898/99 in quite an extraordinary fashion. Rangers won all 18 of their league fixtures, scoring 79 goals and conceding just 18 to complete the perfect season and set a world record only equalled by Hungary's Ferencvaros and Nacional of Uruguay.

It sparked a run of four consecutive league title successes under the club's first manager, William Wilton – the first such run of multiple

witnessed before in the 1920s and 1930s. Under the iron rule of manager Bill Struth they won 15 championships from 1920 to 1939 and were leading in the 1939/40 title race when League football was shut down due to the outbreak of the Second World War.

Football reappeared in a regional format during wartime and Rangers won all seven of the Southern League titles on offer, but these successes are not considered official.

Unsurprisingly, therefore, Rangers won three of the first four post-war

All the prizes were secured by Walter Smith in the 1992/93 season, which was the zenith of the Nine in a Row run, while Dick Advocaat claimed the lot in his debut season of 1998/99, famously defeating Celtic 3–0 at Celtic Park to claim the championship.

Arguably more impressive was the clean sweep achieved by Alex McLeish in 2002/03, when Rangers lifted the title on the final day of the season on goal difference from Celtic to give Rangers their 50th title.

A panoramic view of the 2011 league flag ceremony.

wins – and Rangers had quickly established themselves as the best team in the land.

As is regularly proven, success can be cyclical and Rangers had to wait until the 1910/11 season before they lifted the title again and promptly defended it for the following two seasons. They then dominated Scottish football in a manner that had not been

titles and in 1948/49 became the first Scottish team to win the Treble of League Championship, Scottish Cup and League Cup.

Remarkably, Rangers have achieved the clean sweep seven times in their history. Scot Symon's stylish and spirited side were Treble winners in 1963/64, then Jock Wallace's squad swept all before them in 1976 and 1978.

Two years later the season's end was even more dramatic when Celtic lost at Motherwell and Rangers triumphed at Easter Road when the helicopter carrying the SPL trophy changed direction and headed to Edinburgh.

Walter Smith then returned to deliver three superb championship wins in succession in 2009, 2010 and 2011.

Rangers were dominant in the 1920s and made it five titles in six years with their success in 1924/25, edging Hibs by three points. Back (from left) shows the club's directors – Ex-Baillie Duncan Graham J.P, OBE, W.G. Small, John McPherson, ex-Baillie Joseph Buchanan J.P. (chairman), James Bowie, W.R. Simpson (secretary). Middle – Sandy Archibald, Geordie Henderson, Bert Manderson, Willie Robb, Tully Craig, Andy Cunningham, Arthur Dixon, Davie Meiklejohn. Front – Bill Struth (manager), Willie McCandless, Tommy Muirhead, Tom Cairns (captain), Alan Morton, John Jamieson, George Livingston (trainer). Archibald, Meiklejohn, Muirhead, Cairns and Morton are all wearing their Scotland caps while Manderson has his Ireland cap on.

The Light Blues became the first team to win the Treble in season 1948/49, following the introduction of the League Cup, with a team that boasted the formidable Iron Curtain defence of Bobby Brown, George Young, Jock Shaw, Ian McColl, Willie Woodburn and Sammy Cox and also the attacking flair of Willie Waddell, Willie Thornton and Jimmy Duncanson. The reserve players are pictured in the away kit – blue and white hoops! Rangers promptly won a League and Cup Double the following season as the shot below indicates.

Left: This fantastic collection shows how Championship medals have changed over the years and includes the first ever title win. They are as follows: top row (l-r) Richard Gough 1991–92, Bob McPhail 1929–30, Bob McPhail 1933–34; middle row – Richard Gough 1989–90, David Reid 1890–91, Davie Meiklejohn 1934–35; bottom row – Bob McPhail 1938–39, Bob McPhail 1936–37.

Having taken over from the legendary Bill Struth in 1954,
Scot Symon effectively built two Rangers teams; the
second of which, in the early 1960s, remains an iconic line-up
for so many supporters. The top picture shows the Double-
winning squad from the 1962/63 season, while the second
shot is of the Treble-winning group from season 1963/64.

To win all three domestic trophies in one season is a fantastic feat – to do it twice in three years is quite extraordinary, but that's what Jock Wallace did in 1975/76 and in 1977/78. The top picture shows the class of 1976 while the second shot is from the summer of 1978 with John Greig at the helm, after he replaced Wallace, and Rangers in their new strip.

The wait was long and painful but the moment was so sweet when Rangers became Champions again in 1987 – nine years after their previous success. Chairman David Holmes was instrumental in it all with his sensational move to bring in Graeme Souness as manager who, in turn, made Terry Butcher his captain. His wife Betty unfurled the league flag to the delight of the Ibrox legions.

Nine in a Row
1988/89

The glory road began on August 13, 1988 at Hamilton with a 2–0 win and the title was clinched with a 4–0 win over Hearts at Ibrox on April 29, 1989. Highlights were 5–1 and 4–1 crushing wins over Celtic, and Rangers finished six points clear of Aberdeen.

Nine in a Row
1989/90

Maurice Johnston was the stunning summer signing and he finished top scorer with 15 goals. A 3–0 April Fool's Day win over Celtic sent Rangers on their way and a Trevor Steven header at Tannadice on April 21, 1990 clinched the title. The Dons were runners-up, seven points behind.

Nine in a Row
1990/91

Graeme Souness sensationally quit in April for Liverpool and the title race went to a final day shoot-out with Aberdeen, who only needed a draw to be champions. Two Mark Hateley goals sealed the deal for new boss Walter Smith on a day few will ever forget.

Rangers lost just once in a 24-match spell and clinched the title with three games to spare with a 4–0 home victory over St Mirren. They scored more than a century of goals for the first time since 1939, with Ally McCoist scoring 34 of them, and left runners-up Hearts nine points adrift.

Nine in a Row
1991/92

The zenith of Nine in a Row produced Rangers' fifth Treble. After drawing with Celtic 1–1 at Ibrox in August they did not lose for seven months, stringing together a run of 44 games in all competitions, and came within 90 minutes of the Champions League Final.

Nine in a Row
1992/93

Ravaged by injuries, this was the toughest campaign of all, but inspired by Hateley and aided by the signing of Gordon Durie the Light Blues pipped the Dons by three points and missed out on back-to-back Trebles when they lost 1–0 to Dundee United in the Cup Final.

Nine in a Row
1993/94

Nine in a Row
1994/95

The fans were in awe as Brian Laudrup lit up Scottish football with his sublime skills after Smith's stunning coup to sign him from Fiorentina. A 14-game unbeaten run after a 3–1 Old Firm win set the tone for triumph with Alex McLeish's Motherwell finishing 15 points back in second place.

Nine in a Row
1995/96

Smith shocked the world by signing Paul Gascoigne from Lazio and the Geordie genius was sensational and often controversial. He produced one of the great solo performances with an incredible hat-trick against Aberdeen to hold off nearest challengers Celtic, who lost just once all season.

Nine in a Row
1996/97

History was made in an incredibly fraught campaign. Rangers won all four Old Firm games for the first time in the Premier Division and it was Laudrup who won Nine in a Row with a bullet header at Tannadice. Captain Richard Gough said, 'The boys are legends now.'

Terry
Butcher

Terry Butcher admires
the silverware in 1989.

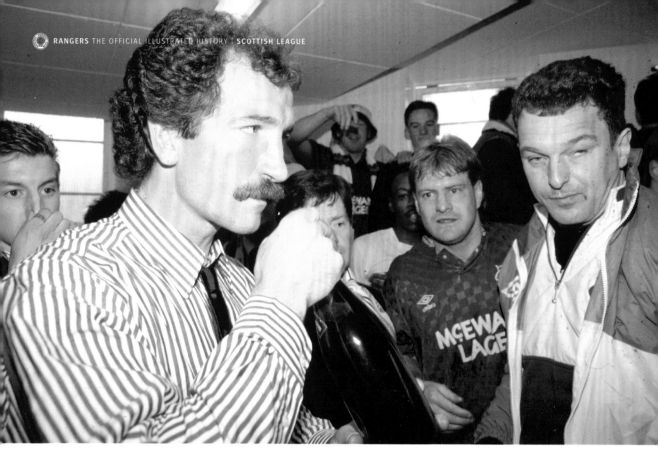

Graeme Souness goes for the bubbly in 1989 ... and Ally McCoist, Ian Durrant and Ian Ferguson are having a bath in 1990!

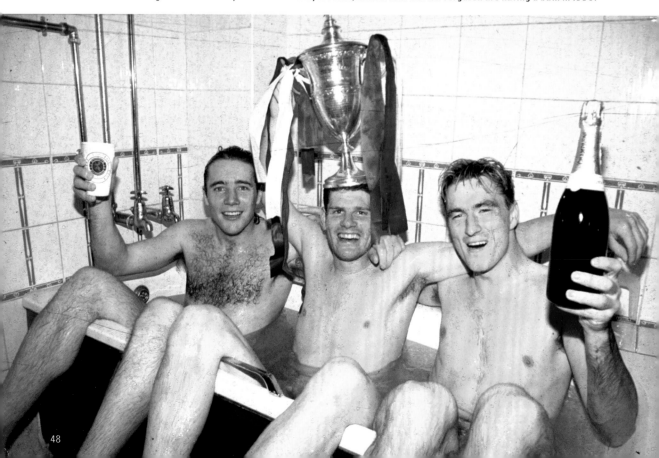

It's bedlam at Ibrox in 1991 as Ian Durrant races to join
Mo Johnston and Mark Hateley in celebration when
Rangers beat Aberdeen to win the title on the final day.

Mo Johnson can't hide his delight after helping Rangers win the title in 1990.

Scottish Champions (54)

*1891, 1899, 1900, 1901, 1902, 1911, 1912, 1913, 1918, 1920, 1921, 1923, 1924, 1925, 1927, 1928, 1929, 1930, 1931, 1933, 1934, 1935, 1937, 1939, 1947, 1949, 1950, 1953, 1956, 1957, 1959, 1961, 1963, 1964, 1975, 1976, 1978, 1987, 1989, 1990, 1991, 1992, 1993, 1994, 1995, 1996, 1997, 1999, 2000, 2003, 2005, 2009, 2010, 2011

*In 1891 the championship was shared with Dumbarton

Captain Terry Butcher seems as mad as a hatter as he celebrates at Tannadice in 1989.

Stuart McCall gets into the party spirit after clinching four in a row at Broomfield in 1993.

Ally McCoist and Trevor Steven fill the cup as Archie Knox looks on in 1994.

It was party time at Tannadice in 1997 as Gazza, Derek McInnes, Ally McCoist and Gordon Durie celebrate Nine in a Row.

Walter Smith claimed his first title in the stunning final day triumph of 1991 and (left) celebrates the 1992 triumph with assistant Archie Knox.

The inimitable Paul Gascoigne was
the star of the Eight in a Row party.

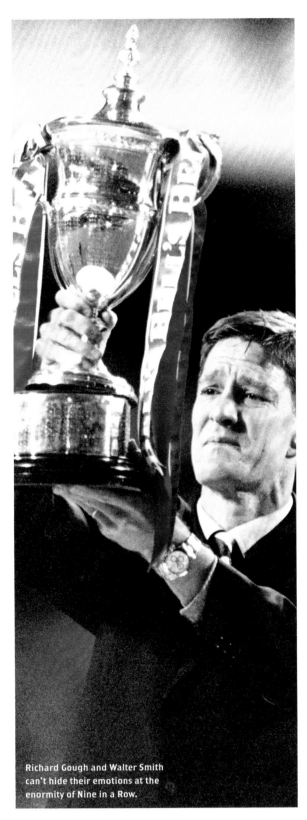

Richard Gough and Walter Smith can't hide their emotions at the enormity of Nine in a Row.

Rod Wallace, Jorg Albertz and Neil McCann display the spoils of the remarkable 1998/99 campaign when Dutch manager Dick Advocaat swept the boards in his first season in charge. Wallace finished the season as top scorer and scored the winner in the Scottish Cup Final, while Albertz and McCann were the men who got the goals as Rangers won the title at Parkhead, hammering Celtic 3–0.

Alex McLeish won two titles as Rangers' manager – 2003 and 2005 – and both campaigns went to the final day.
Mikel Arteta (above left) scored with a penalty to ensure the 2003 crown as Rangers beat Dunfermline 6–1 to hold off
Celtic on goal difference. Then in 2005 the helicopter carrying the SPL trophy changed direction and headed
for Easter Road when Rangers beat Hibs to finish clear of Celtic, who crashed to defeat at Motherwell.

The renaissance of Rangers under Walter Smith between 2007 and 2011 was remarkable, with a hat-trick of titles. The first victory came at Tannadice in May 2009 when goals from Pedro Mendes, Kyle Lafferty and Kris Boyd swept Dundee United away 3–0 on the final day of the season.

The 2009/10 campaign produced a convincing title triumph as Rangers clinched the crown at Easter Road on April 25 and were then presented with the trophy in their final home game on May 9.

EXIT 12

Clydesdale Bank

CB Clydesdale Bank PREMIER LEAGUE

CHAMPIONS

Ally McCoist celebrates with the Rangers fans at Tannadice in his own inimitable style after the last-day title win of 2009.

Walter Smith and Davie Weir lead the celebrations at Kilmarnock in 2011 when Rangers made it Three in a Row.

John Greig, a Treble-winner in 1964, 1976 and 1978, congratulates Barry Ferguson who achieved a clean sweep as Rangers captain in 2003.

Walter Smith, flanked by lieutenants Ally McCoist and Kenny McDowall, show off the SPL trophy and Scottish Cup after a memorable Double-winning campaign in 2008/09.

Chapter 4
Scottish Cup

1928 Scottish Cup final team

THE **Homecoming Scotland** SCOTTISH CUP

WINNERS 2009

FROM Davie Meiklejohn's crucial penalty through Tom Forsyth's tap-in, Davie Cooper's wizardry and Brian Laudrup's masterclass to Nacho Novo's wonder goal, Rangers have been at the hub of the greatest moments **in Scottish Cup history ...**

Winners of the trophy 33 times and losing finalists on 17 occasions, the Light Blues have been regularly dominant in Scottish football's oldest competition – but they have equally suffered considerable disappointment.

After four wins at the turn of the 19th century, Rangers incredibly went 25 years without lifting the trophy until April 14, 1928 when the hoodoo was finally smashed.

A then-record crowd of 118,115 saw Meiklejohn score from the spot after Celtic captain Willie McStay had handled the ball on the line, and it sent Rangers on

their way to a memorable 4–0 win and a League and Cup Double for the first time in their history.

The trophy scarcely left Ibrox in the years that followed, with five successes, including three in a row, up until 1936 with the 5–0 crushing of St Mirren in 1935 – the most impressive and also Rangers' record final win in the competition.

In the aftermath of the Second World War, Rangers, featuring their famous Iron Curtain defence, sealed another hat-trick of victories. The second of these – the 1948/49 win – was significant as it was part of the first Treble won by a Scottish club.

Billy Simpson fatefully sealed the 1953 Final replay against Aberdeen, having been left out of the first game by disciplinarian manager Bill Struth for being sent off in a league match a week earlier.

clinched the Treble for the second time. Two years later Dane Kai Johansen become the first foreign player to score the winner in a final when Celtic were beaten 1–0 in a replay.

It was another seven years before Rangers got their hands on the trophy. In an epic 3–2 win over Celtic, Forsyth famously scuffed the ball home from six inches after Derek Parlane's header had hit the inside of the left post and run along the line.

However, it was 11 painful years before Rangers were victorious once more when Airdrie were beaten 2–1 and Ally McCoist claimed his one and only Scottish Cup medal.

The 2–1 win over Aberdeen the following season gave Rangers the Treble for the fifth time. Walter Smith then claimed victory again in 1996 when Laudrup completely destroyed Hearts and Gordon Durie became the first Rangers player to score a hat-trick in a final in the 5–1 win.

Rangers had to wait seven years before they won again. It was a sweet moment for stalwart Ian McColl who was recalled in the twilight of his career for the 2–0 win over Kilmarnock to collect his fifth winners' medal.

There was another hat-trick of wins between 1962 and 1964, the third of which, a 3–1 win over Dundee,

Victories over Hearts in 1976 and Aberdeen in 1978 were hugely significant as they gave

Jock Wallace a clean sweep of honours on each occasion.

The 4–1 replay win over Dundee United in 1981 was made memorable by the mesmerising performance of Davie Cooper.

Treble No. 6 was secured when Rod Wallace settled the 1999 final, while Lorenzo Amoruso gave Alex McLeish a clean sweep in 2003 with his winning header against Dundee.

Rangers last won the Cup in 2009 and it was fans' favourite Nacho Novo who clinched the victory with an outlandish long-range shot against Falkirk.

Chairman Joseph Buchanan proudly clutches the Scottish Cup after Rangers' success in 1932. The Light Blues needed a replay before seeing off Kilmarnock 3–0 with goals from Jimmy Fleming, Bob McPhail and Sam English. Incredibly the two matches with Killie produced a combined attendance of 217,657. Back – Bobby Main, Bob McPhail, Bob McAuley, Tom Hamilton, Jimmy Simpson, Jimmy Fleming, William Rogers Simpson (director), Sandy Archibald, Jimmy 'Doc' Marshall, Davie Meiklejohn, Duncan Graham (director). Front – Dougie Gray, Bill Struth (manager), Joseph Buchanan (chairman), George Brown, Alan Morton, Sam English.

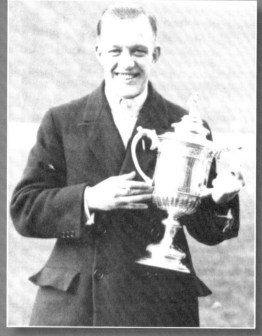

No wonder Davie Meiklejohn is smiling as he holds the Cup after the 1928 final; Rangers had not won it for 25 years but they certainly smashed the winless run in style with a 4–0 triumph over Celtic. It was Meiklejohn who set up the historic win with a vital penalty, then Bob McPhail (above right and hidden in the second picture on the right) scored while Sandy Archibald grabbed two goals.

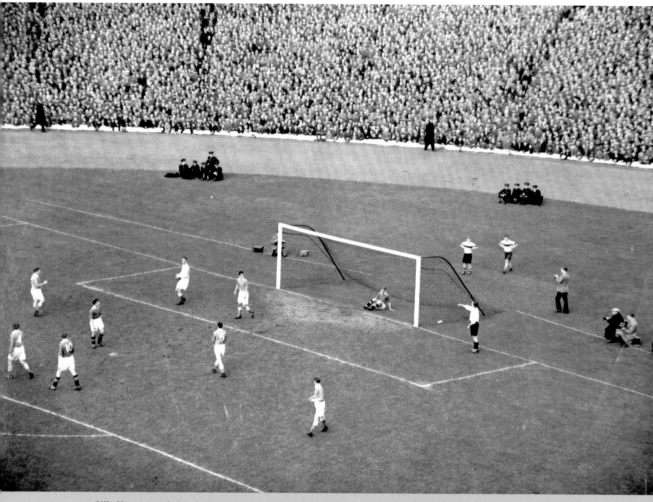

Billy Simpson ended up in the Aberdeen net in this photograph but thankfully the Ulsterman also put the ball there in the 1953 Cup Final replay. Simpson had been left out of the first match by disciplinarian Bill Struth for being sent off in a league match but returned to score the only goal.

The Rangers Scottish Cup team of 1929-30. *Back row, left to right:* Meiklejohn, Marshall, Archibald, Fleming, T. Hamilton, Buchanan, Craig. *Front, left to right:* J. Kerr (trainer), Brown, Gray, McDonald, Muirhead, McPhail, R. Hamilton, Nicholson, Morton, W. Struth (manager)

This is the team that won the Cup in 1930. They defeated Partick Thistle 2–1 in a replay – with Doc Marshall and Tully Craig scoring – after a goal-less first game.

1951.

When the Scottish Cup was won three seasons in succession—1947-48, 1948-49, 1949-50—these eleven players took part in all three Cup competitions.
Back Row (left to right)—W. Waddell, Ian McColl, Geo. Young, Robt. Brown, W. Woodburn, S. Cox.
Sitting—W. Williamson, W. Thornton, J. Shaw, J. Duncanson, E. Rutherford.

Scottish Cup Winners (33)

1894, 1897, 1898, 1903, 1928, 1930, 1932, 1934, 1935, 1936, 1948,
1949, 1950, 1953, 1960, 1962, 1963, 1964, 1966, 1973, 1976, 1978, 1979,
1981, 1992, 1993, 1996, 1999, 2000, 2002, 2003, 2008, 2009

The early sixties was a golden period for Rangers. Led by Eric Caldow, they comfortably won the 1962 Cup Final when St Mirren were beaten 2–0.

Resplendent in blue and white stripes, Rangers won the Treble for the second time when they beat Dundee 3–1 in the epic 1964 Scottish Cup Final which was clinched in the final moments by Jimmy Millar, who had scored earlier in the game, and Ralph Brand. The happy players are Billy Ritchie, Davie Provan, Ronnie McKinnon, Bobby Shearer (with the Cup), George McLean, Jimmy Miller, John Greig, Jim Baxter. Front – Willie Henderson and Davie Wilson.

Skipper Bobby Shearer is held aloft by Davie Provan and Davie Wilson as Rangers celebrate the 1964 Cup final triumph at their usual venue, the St Enoch's Hotel in Glasgow.

Tom Forsyth famously scores the winner in 1973.

Stalwart Ian McColl captained the side in 1960 and is also pictured with Ian McMillan, Johnny Little and Sammy Baird.

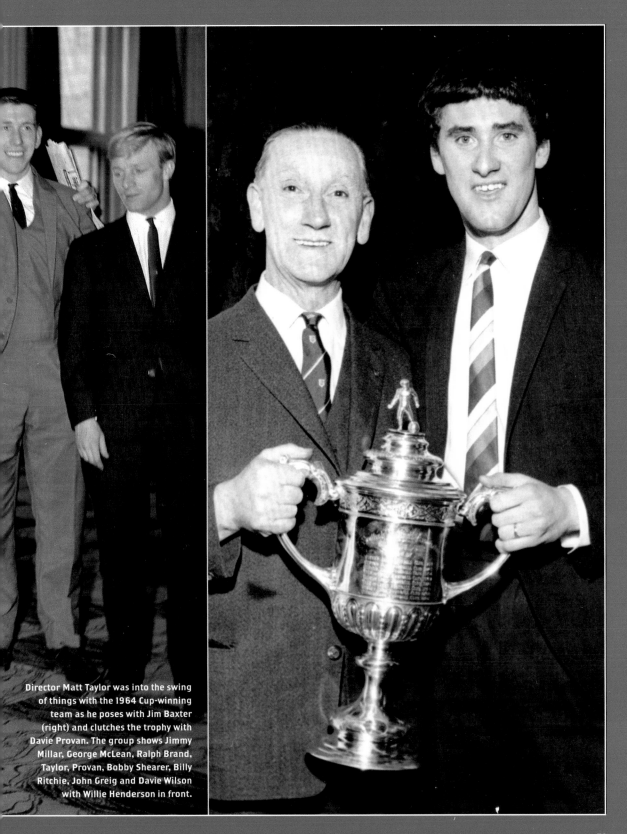

Director Matt Taylor was into the swing of things with the 1964 Cup-winning team as he poses with Jim Baxter (right) and clutches the trophy with Davie Provan. The group shows Jimmy Millar, George McLean, Ralph Brand, Taylor, Provan, Bobby Shearer, Billy Ritchie, John Greig and Davie Wilson with Willie Henderson in front.

John Greig and Jock Wallace are joyous on the Hampden turf after the 3–1 Cup Final win over Hearts in 1976 gave Rangers the Treble for the third time in their history. Watching on is Johnny Hamilton.

FACT: Dazzling winger Alec Smith, who played for Rangers for 21 years between 1894 and 1915, holds the Rangers record of 74 appearances in the Scottish Cup although he only won it three times.

Rangers had not won the Cup for 11 years when Walter Smith's side beat Airdrie 2–1 in 1992.

Archie Knox celebrates on the team bus.

Walter Smith celebrates the Cup win with sons Neil and Steven and wife Ethel.

Andy Goram gazes in wonderment as Richard Gough lifts
the trophy after the 5–1 mauling of Hearts in 1996.

Hat-trick hero Gordon Durie celebrates
with Paul Gascoigne in 1996.

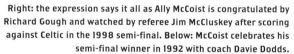

Right: the expression says it all as Ally McCoist is congratulated by
Richard Gough and watched by referee Jim McCluskey after scoring
against Celtic in the 1998 semi-final. Below: McCoist celebrates his
semi-final winner in 1992 with coach Davie Dodds.

Rangers celebrated a memorable 3–2 Scottish Cup win over Celtic on May 4, 2002 when Peter Lovenkrands sealed the deal in the last minute.

Lorenzo Amoruso plays the Jester role to a tee!

Ferguson celebrates the famous triumph with Arthur Numan.

Captain Barry Ferguson rips his shirt off after scoring a stunning free kick to level the final at 2-2, with Craig Moore in hot pursuit.

Shota Arveladze gets into the party spirit at Hampden.

Arthur Numan salutes the fans after his last game for Rangers in the 2003 Cup final, helped
by Fernando Ricksen, Ronald de Boer, Shota Arveladze and Michael Mols.

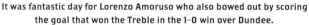

It was fantastic day for Lorenzo Amoruso who also bowed out by scoring
the goal that won the Treble in the 1–0 win over Dundee.

Rod Wallace settled the 1999 Cup final to give Dick Advocaat a Treble in his first season with the only goal against Celtic.

Derek McInnes and Jorg Albertz joined in the fun and then kissed the trophy.

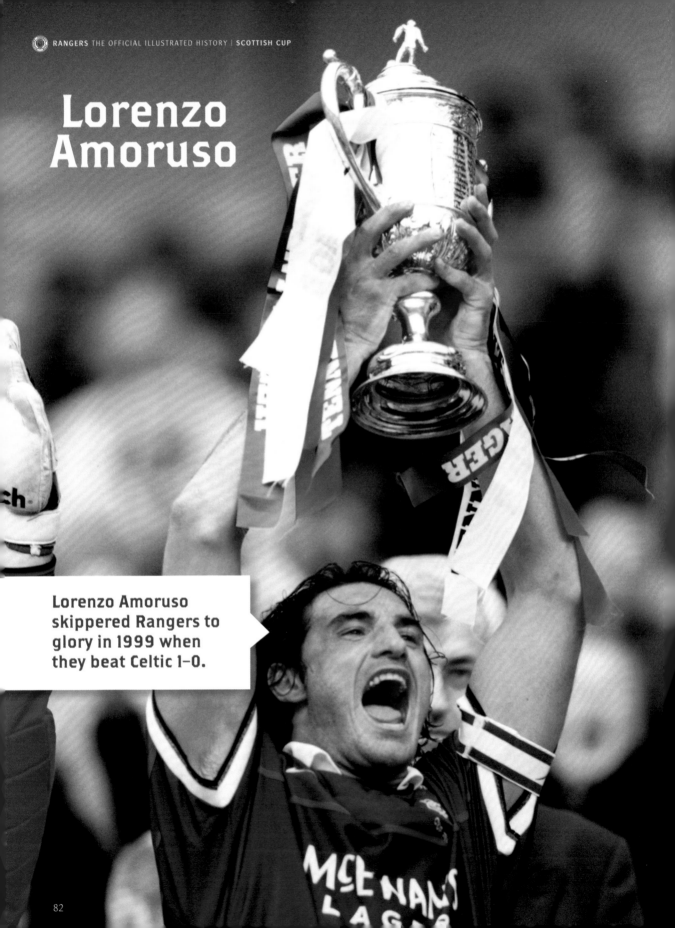

Lorenzo Amoruso

Lorenzo Amoruso skippered Rangers to glory in 1999 when they beat Celtic 1-0.

Alex McLeish celebrates with the fans back at Ibrox after the sensational 2002 win over Celtic.

Nacho Novo's wonder strike settled the 2009 final against Falkirk.

Kris Boyd was the hero with two goals
against Queen of the South in 2008.

Ally McCoist and goal-scorer
DaMarcus Beasley show the
colours after the 2008 triumph.

Chapter 5
League Cup

Naismith and Jelavic celebrate

Richard Gough lifts the trophy in 1993/94.

RANGERS were the first winners of the League Cup when it was introduced in season 1946/47 and they have dominated the competition with unrelenting power by claiming the trophy on 27 occasions in the intervening years.

Indeed, the old three-handled cup has been a regular exhibit in the famous Ibrox trophy room in the last 25 years, in particular when Rangers have won it a remarkable 14 times and also lost in two other finals. When you consider Celtic have only 14 wins to their name, it underlines Rangers' supremacy.

The format and timing of the competition has chopped and changed over the years with an early sectional set-up replaced by a straight knock-out scenario, but almost invariably there have been red, white and blue ribbons around the cup.

After that inaugural success – a 4–0 win over Aberdeen – Rangers won the 1948/49 final when they beat Raith Rovers 2–0 with goals from Torry Gillick and Willie Paton to claim part of the first ever Treble in Scottish football.

Strangely, more than a decade passed before Rangers got their hands on the trophy again and they promptly won it in four of the next five seasons from 1960/61 to 1964/65.

It was a special tournament for Jim Forrest who scored four goals in the 5–0 win over Morton in 1963/64 when Rangers won the

between Jim Craig and Billy McNeill to head the only goal of the Old Firm final in 1970/71 watched by 106,263 spectators.

Johnstone was a major established player when Rangers won the Cup again in the 1975/76 and 1977/78 seasons and swept the boards under Jock Wallace. Both victories were achieved against Celtic with Alex MacDonald heading the only goal on October 25, 1975 and then Davie Cooper and Gordon Smith scoring in the 2–1 win on March 18, 1978.

He scored a hat-trick in the 1983/84 final against Celtic; he scored the clincher from close range in the 3–2 win over Aberdeen in 1988/89; he came off the bench after a long injury to score with an overhead kick to beat Hibs in 1993/94 and he netted a double in the 4–3 win over Hearts in 1996/97.

It was Frenchman Stephane Guivarc'h and German Jorg Albertz who scored the goals in the 2–1 victory over St Johnstone on November 29, 1998, which was the first part of a Treble for manager Dick Advocaat in his first season in charge.

Alex McLeish won the trophy twice and the second success – a 2–1 triumph over Celtic – also constituted part one of a fantastic Treble in season 2002/03.

Walter Smith's second spell as boss produced three victories and all were dramatic. Dundee United were beaten on penalties in 2008. Rangers only had nine men when Kenny Miller scored the winner in 2009 against St Mirren – after Kevin Thomson and Danny Wilson were sent off – while Nikica Jelavic scored an extra-time winner to defeat Celtic 2–1 in 2011.

The scoreboard in 2002.

Treble for the second time – the first time such a scoring feat had been achieved. Then he scored both goals the following season when Celtic were beaten 2–1.

The late 1960s and early 1970s were difficult periods for Rangers but a precocious 16-year-old called Derek Johnstone gave the fans some respite when he jumped

If Johnstone was a key protagonist in some great finals he has nothing on good friend Ally McCoist, who proudly holds NINE winners' medals – a record that may never be surpassed.

His victories came in 1983/84, 1984/85, 1986/87, 1987/88, 1988/89, 1990/91, 1992/93, 1993/94 and 1996/97.

FOOTBALL LEAGU
19 46
1996-97. RANGERS F.C.
1997-98. CELTIC F.C.
1998-99. RANGERS F.C.
1999-00. CELTIC F.C.
2000-01. CELTIC F.C.
2001-02. RANGERS F.C.
2002-03. RANGERS F.C.
The co-operative insurance

The victorious squad from the 2002/03 triumph over Celtic celebrate their success in the Blue Room.

Scottish League Cup Winners (27)

1946/47, 1948/49, 1960/61, 1961/62, 1963/64, 1964/65, 1970/71, 1975/76, 1977/78,
1978/79, 1981/82, 1983/84, 1984/85, 1986/87, 1987/88, 1988/89, 1990/91, 1992/93,
1993/94, 1996/97, 1998/99, 2001/02, 2002/03, 2004/05, 2007/08, 2009/10, 2010/11

Celtic keeper John Fallon is helpless as Jim Forrest sweeps the ball into the net in the 1964/65 Final. Forrest scored both goals in a 2–1 win and set a record of scoring four goals in the previous year's final – a 5–0 win over Morton.

Alex MacDonald had a habit of scoring vital goals in the 1970s and his diving header decided the 1975/76 Final which sent Rangers on their way to a glorious Treble.

Ian Ferguson's greatest moment as a Rangers player came in 1984/85
when his goal defeated Dundee United at Hampden. He is pictured
with Dave McPherson and Craig Paterson on the victory lap.

Ally McCoist's remarkable record in the League Cup began in 1983/84 when he blasted a hat-trick against Celtic – the last time such a feat has been achieved in an Old Firm game – to secure a 3–2 win. In total McCoist won nine medals in the competition.

The victorious 1983/84 team. Back – Dave McPherson, Ally Dawson, Sandy Clark, Bobby Russell, Craig Paterson, Jimmy Nicholl and Davie Cooper. Front – John MacDonald, Hugh Burns, Ally McCoist, John McClelland, Peter McCloy and Colin McAdam.

The 1987/88 final was the first to be decided by penalties after an epic 3–3 draw with Aberdeen. The winning team is (back) Ally McCoist, Derek Ferguson, Richard Gough, Jimmy Nicholl, Ian Durrant, John McGregor, Davie Cooper. Front – Stuart Munro, Graham Roberts, Trevor Francis, Avi Cohen, Nicky Walker, Robert Fleck.

1970/71 League Cup
Final programme.

1978 League Cup
Final programme.

1979 League Cup
semi-final programme.

Richard Gough celebrated his installation as captain with a memorable extra time winner against Celtic in 1990/91 which clinched a 2-1 win. Back – Gough, Mark Hateley, Pieter Huistra, Nigel Spackman, Terry Hurlock, Gary Stevens, Mark Walter, Ally McCoist. Front – Stuart Munro, Chris Woods, Ian Ferguson, Trevor Steven, John Brown.

1980 League Cup programme.

1993/94 League Cup Final programme.

2010/11 League Cup Final programme.

League Cup
OF 1991

Chairman David Murray and manager Graeme Souness celebrated
the 1990/91 League Cup triumph in the Hampden dressing room
with kitman George 'Doddie' Soutar. It was the last major honour
won by Souness, who left to take over Liverpool six months later.

League Cup
OF 1993

There was a fairy-tale finish to the 1993/94 showdown when
Ally McCoist came off the bench to score with an overhead kick
to sink Hibs 2–1, having suffered a broken leg six months earlier.
Blues brother Ian Durrant scored the other Rangers goal.

The first leg of a fantastic Treble in the remarkable 1992/93 season was secured when Aberdeen were beaten 2–1 in the League Cup Final. The happy squad is – Back – Billy Kirkwood (coach), Pieter Huistra, Stuart McCall, Dave McPherson, Davie Robertson, Mark Hateley, Archie Knox (assistant manager), Ian Ferguson, John McGregor (coach). Front – Walter Smith (manager), John Brown, Ally McCoist, Dale Gordon, Davie Dodds (coach), Trevor Steven, Richard Gough, Ally Maxwell, Ian Durrant, Andy Goram.

Dick Advocaat's reign as Rangers
manager got off to a flying start with
victory in the 1998/99 League Cup
Final when St Johnstone were defeated
2–1, and it proved to be part one of an
incredible clean sweep of the honours.
The dramatic change to the squad from
the previous season is all too evident.
Back – Tony Vidmar, Antti Niemi, Arthur
Numan, Giovanni van Bronckhorst, Barry
Ferguson, Sergio Porrini (hidden), Jonatan
Johansson (hidden), Ian Ferguson, Jorg
Albertz, Rod Wallace, Andrei Kanchelskis,
Lorenzo Amoruso, Colin Hendry.

Alex McLeish can't hide his joy as Rangers make the victory journey back to Ibrox after the sensational 2–1 victory over Celtic in March 2003. Claudio Caniggia and Peter Lovenkrands scored the goals and John Hartson missed a last-minute penalty which would have forced extra time. Remarkably there were nine different nationalities in Rangers' starting line-up: Stefan Klos (German); Fernando Ricksen (Dutch), Lorenzo Amoruso (Italian), Craig Moore (Australian), Jerome Bonnissel (French); Caniggia (Argentinean), Barry Ferguson (British), Mikel Arteta (Spanish), Lovenkrands (Danish), Ronald de Boer, Michael Mols (Dutch).

Captain Barry Ferguson and manager Alex McLeish show off the
trophy in the Blue Room after the 2002/03 victory over Celtic.

Match winner Nikica Jelavic and manager Walter Smith can't hide their delight after the 2–1 extra-time win over Celtic in 2011.

Kenny Miller spins away in sheer delight after scoring the winner in the incredible 2009/10 final against St Mirren. Rangers won 1–0 despite having Kevin Thomson and Danny Wilson sent off.

Chapter 6

Europe

Barcelona '72 – Johnston Scores

THERE is nothing quite like the drama, power and excitement of top-class European action, and Rangers have been at the heart of it all for nearly 60 years.

The 2008 UEFA Cup Final team – back – Sasa Papac, Steven Whittaker, Brahim Hemdani, Neil Alexander, Davie Weir, Carlos Cuellar – front – Jean-Claude Darcheville, Kirk Broadfoot, Barry Ferguson, Kevin Thomson, Steve Davis.

Only Real Madrid, Barcelona, Sporting Lisbon and Anderlecht have appeared in Europe more often than the Light Blues, which is a sign of the club's remarkable consistency.

Rangers have been ground-breakers in so many instances. Hibs were Scotland's first representatives in the European Cup in 1955 when they were invited after champions Aberdeen declined to take part, but Rangers led the way from the following year.

The Light Blues played four seasons in European competition – including a final – before Celtic played their first Euro match. They were the first British side to reach a major European final when they lost out 4–1 on aggregate to Fiorentina in the inaugural Cup Winners' Cup in 1960/61. (Birmingham City played in the representative Inter-Cities Fairs

Cup Final the year before.) They instigated the setting up of the Super Cup in 1973, they were the first British side to play in the Champions League in 1992/93, and in 2005/06 became the first Scottish club to progress from the group phase of Europe's premier tournament.

Of course the crowning glory of their involvement at this level was the fantastic European Cup Winners' Cup triumph of 1972, when they defeated Moscow Dynamo 3–2 in the Nou Camp Stadium, Barcelona.

Derek Johnstone, Dave Smith, Tommy McLean, Alfie Conn, Colin Stein, Alex MacDonald and Willie Johnston.

Rangers have been involved in two other major finals but both ended in disappointment.

They lost the 1967 Cup Winners' Cup final to Bayern Munich 1–0 in extra time in Nuremburg, which was like a home game for the German giants.

In season 2007/08 with Walter Smith at the helm they embarked

Fairs Cup in 1968/69. Outwith that, Smith led the Light Blues to within an ace of the inaugural Champions League Final in 1992/93 when they completed 10 matches unbeaten, but they were edged out by Olympique Marseille who defeated AC Milan in the final. The fact that the French side was subsequently prevented from defending the trophy following bribery and corruption charges domestically only rubbed salt into the wounds.

Advocaat can boast the most consistent European record of all

Colin Stein scores against Sporting Lisbon in 1971.

Kirk Broadfoot celebrates Nacho Novo's penalty in Florence in 2008.

In a sensational run Rangers knocked out Rennes, Sporting Lisbon, Torino and the mightily impressive Bayern Munich to go on and become kings of Europe in Catalonia.

The men who wrote their names into Rangers lore that night were: Peter McCloy, Sandy Jardine, Willie Mathieson, John Greig,

on a remarkable 19-game adventure which culminated at the City of Manchester Stadium, where they lost 2–0 in the UEFA Cup final to Zenit St Petersburg, ironically coached by former manager Dick Advocaat.

Rangers can also claim semi-final appearances in the European Cup in 1959/60 and the revamped

Rangers' managers in that he bossed roughly a dozen matches in each of his four campaigns. Having said that he was undoubtedly aided by a handsome budget which, it was hoped, would produce more tangible success. There is scarcely anything more powerful than a major European night at Ibrox and Rangers have hosted so many of them over the years.

Rangers' captain Jock Shaw and his team line up before a friendly with Moscow Dynamo in 1945.

Eric Caldow exchanging gifts with Fiorentina captain Alberto Orzan in the second leg of the Cup Winners' Cup Final in 1961.

Johnny Hubbard in action in a friendly against Valencia in 1955.

John Greig leads Rangers out to face Bayern Munich in the 1967 Cup Winners' Cup Final, with Norrie Martin behind him and Sepp Maier and Franz Beckenbauer to his right.

Ronnie McKinnon battles with Newcastle's Wyn Davies in the semi-finals of the Fairs Cup in 1969.

Roger Hynd had a goal disallowed in the 1967 Final, won 1–0 by Bayern.

The 1967 European Cup Winners' Cup Final team group.
Back – Sandy Jardine, Kai Johansen, Norrie Martin, Davie Provan, Ronnie McKinnon, John Greig.
Front – Willie Henderson, Alex Smith, Roger Hynd, Dave Smith, Willie Johnston.

John Greig shakes hands with Rennes' captain Louis Cardiet in 1971.

Colin Stein gets in a header against Rennes in 1971.

Rangers celebrate the fantastic 2–0 victory over Bayern Munich which sent them into the 1972
European Cup Winners' Cup Final. Back – Derek Parlane, Derek Johnstone, Colin Stein,
Alex MacDonald, Graham Fyfe, Alfie Conn, Gerry Neef. Middle – Peter McCloy, Willie Johnson,
Dave Smith, Tommy McLean, Willie Mathieson, Alex Miller, Ronnie McKinnon.
Front – Sandy Jardine, John Greig, Colin Jackson.

Colin Stein was a pivotal man against
Sporting Lisbon in the second round
scoring twice at Ibrox (above) and twice in
the Portuguese capital (below right).

Alfie Conn in action against Sporting at Ibrox in what was an epic tie.

Willie Henderson is hidden from view as his ferocious shot hits the Sporting net at Ibrox.

Torino clear their lines against Rangers in the quarter-finals of the Cup Winners' Cup' in March 1972.

Colin Stein challenges Sepp Maier against Bayern in April 1972.

Willie Johnston in action against Torino in 1972.

Derek Parlane (ground) scores against Bayern as Franz Beckenbauer looks on in April 1972.

Derek Parlane and Tommy McLean celebrate against Bayern.

John Greig goes through the pre-match ritual with Moscow Dynamo captain Yozhev Sabo before the Cup Winners' Cup Final on May 24, 1972.

Colin Stein wheels away in joy after scoring the first goal against the Russians.

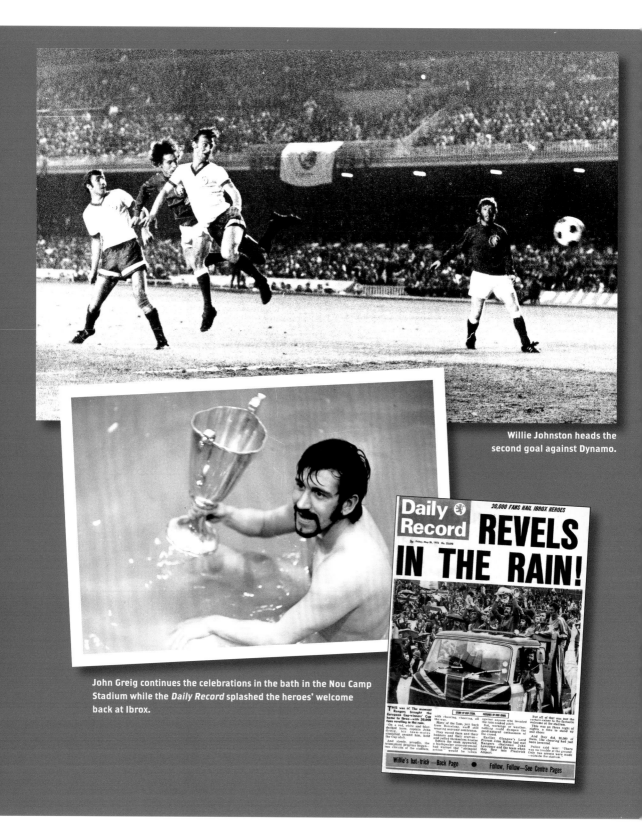

Willie Johnston heads the
second goal against Dynamo.

John Greig continues the celebrations in the bath in the Nou Camp
Stadium while the *Daily Record* splashed the heroes' welcome
back at Ibrox.

There were fantastic scenes at Ibrox when the team paraded the trophy to the supporters after their historic European triumph in Barcelona.

The victorious team that won the 1972 Cup Winners' Cup. Back – Willie Waddell (manager), Jock Wallace (assistant manager), Colin Stein, Alfie Conn, Derek Johnstone, Peter McCloy, Dave Smith, Sandy Jardine, Willie Mathieson, Tom Craig (physiotherapist) Front – Tommy McLean, John Greig, Alex MacDonald, Willie Johnston.

The whole squad got together again in 2002. Back – Tom Craig (physiotherapist), Gerry Neef, Alex Miller, Derek Parlane, Jim Denny, Willie Johnston. Middle – Derek Johnstone, Colin Jackson, Ronnie McKinnon, Alfie Conn, Willie Mathieson, Peter McCloy, Colin Stein, Dave Smith, Willie Henderson. Front – Graham Fyfe, Alex MacDonald, John Greig, Sandy Jardine, Stan Anderson (reserve coach).

Rangers had varying fortunes in the Champions League in the 1990s but there were some fantastic nights. Jorg Albertz shoots against Ajax in 1996.

Brian Laudrup in action against Alania Vladikavkaz in 1996. Rangers beat the Russian champions 10-3 on aggregate.

Mark Hateley in action against Marseille in 1992.

Ian Durrant surges against Bruges in 1992.

Barry Ferguson leads the celebrations as Rangers reach the last 16 of the Champions League 2005/06 after a 1–1 draw with Inter Milan.

The fans go wild in
El Madrigal after
Peter Lovenkrands
scored in the 1–1 draw
with Villarreal in the
last 16 of the Champions
League in 2006.

123

The European adventure in the 2007/08 season was quite extraordinary as Rangers under Walter Smith needed two qualifying ties to reach the Champions League group phase where they faced Barcelona, as our shot of Nacho Novo challenging Iniesta shows. They then parachuted into the UEFA Cup and the momentum really began to build.

An away goals win over Panathinaikos, a fantastic show of resilience in Bremen and then a wonderful night in Lisbon when Rangers beat Sporting 2–0, led to the semi-finals where Fiorentina lay in wait. After 210 goal-less minutes the tie went to penalties and it was Nacho Novo who slammed the decisive kick to send Rangers to the 2008 UEFA Cup Final.

Walter Smith prepares for the biggest match of his career at the City of Manchester Stadium.

Smith was able to share some pre-match fun with Dick Advocaat but sadly it was the Dutchman who was the happier after the final whistle with his Zenit St Petersburg winning 2–0. However, the 19-game run had been an unbelievable adventure.

Chapter 7
Ibrox

A view from the Bill Struth Main Stand

IBROX Stadium is the last word in state-of-the-art sports venues and Rangers are justly proud of owning one of the leading grounds in the world.

But unlike many other football clubs, Rangers have preserved all that is valuable of the old and combined it with the best of the new.

Inside are four magnificent stands, plush executive suites, conference rooms, jumbotron television screens and a superb restaurant. Outside, along Edmiston Drive, the sweep of the imposing red-brick building presents the visitor with the grandeur of a bygone age.

It is a far cry from those windy public pitches on Flesher's Haugh at Glasgow Green where

Rangers played their first matches in 1872. It was three years before the club had their first home, a field at Burnbank.

Within a year they had moved to Clydesdale's ground at Kinning Park and then the club moved to Govan and the original Ibrox Stadium in 1887, which is located where Edmiston House now stands.

Two years later they moved 100 yards to the current site of Ibrox. Rangers' first match at the new stadium was a 3–1 victory over Hearts in the Inter-City League on December 30, 1899.

Within a few months a grandstand seating 4,500 was opened and the club could boast two covered enclosures. The second was opposite the grandstand, where the present Govan Stand is now located, and became known as the Bovril Stand because of the large advertisement displayed on its roof.

A sum of £20,000 had been spent on the stadium – a substantial amount for those days – and the capacity had reached 75,000.

Behind the goals at each end were scaffolding terraces, consisting of wooden planks on an iron frame. The terraces that stood on the site of the present Broomloan Road Stand rose up 150 feet.

Because of its size, the ground was awarded the Scotland v England international match in 1902. But at this game, the first Ibrox disaster occurred when a section of the wooden terracing collapsed and 26 people were tragically killed.

One consequence of the disaster was the decision that solid earth banking would provide a safer basis for terracing. The wooden scaffolds were removed and the ground capacity was cut to 25,000.

Construction engineer Archibald Leitch, who had worked on

Hampden Park and Everton's Goodison Park, was called in to advise Rangers. By 1910, Ibrox Stadium had taken on the shape of a vast bowl and had expanded to accommodate 63,000 fans.

After the First World War, the capacity was again improved to take crowds in excess of 80,000 and by the 1920s the club was on the way to building what was undoubtedly one of the finest stadia in Britain.

The centrepiece was Leitch's magnificent grandstand which included the club's offices, the marble staircase, new dressing rooms and a kit room. The grandstand, set off by a façade which is now a listed building, was opened for the New Year match against Celtic on January 1, 1929 which Rangers won 3–0.

Indeed, the Old Firm game of January 2, 1939 set what is still the British record attendance for a League game when 118,567 watched Rangers beat Celtic 2–1 at Ibrox Stadium.

There were no major structural changes to the stadium for the next 30 years, although legislation limited crowds to around 80,000. However, it was another Old Firm game, the fateful one on January 2, 1971, when 66 people died in the second Ibrox disaster when a terrible crush developed, that was the catalyst for Rangers' ground to become all-seated.

Manager Willie Waddell had the vision. He believed that steep terracing and exits, such as the one where the disaster happened on Staircase 13, had to go. He visited Borussia Dortmund's Westfalen Stadium for ideas and began to lay the foundations for the changes which culminated in today's Ibrox Stadium.

In 1973, 10,000 bench seats were fitted on the north terracing as a temporary measure, becoming known as the Centenary Stand. By 1978 the east terracing was being ripped up and a year later the Copland Road Stand was in its place. The Govan and Broomloan Stands followed.

A top deck was added to the Main Stand in 1991 and the last standing areas were replaced by seats. The stadium is now completely enclosed and the ground's capacity is 51,082, following the addition of Bar 72 in the summer of 2006 which added three rows to the top tier of the Govan Stand.

Of course Ibrox is a treasure trove with many wonderful trophies, mementoes and gifts in the Trophy Room and other hospitality areas.

However, for all supporters it is a temple of dreams, where so many great players have achieved so much glory and success for the club.

A floodlit view of the magnificent façade of the Bill Struth Main Stand at Ibrox, which is a listed building.

Some original share certificates which are on display at Ibrox.

This oil painting of Bill Struth takes pride of place in the Trophy Room, and below
is the typewriter used by the legendary manager.

The Trophy Room at Ibrox is a treasure trove of silverware, memorabilia and gifts from other clubs.

The Arsenal cannon.

The grasshopper from Zurich.

The collapse of the terracing at the Scotland–England game in 1902 claimed the lives of 26 people and forced the reconstruction at Ibrox.

A view of a more modern Ibrox with the old Press Box perched on top of the Main Stand.

The façade at Ibrox has scarcely changed since this photograph was taken in the 1930s.

The Valencia Trophy, one of the many items of memorabilia in the Trophy Room.

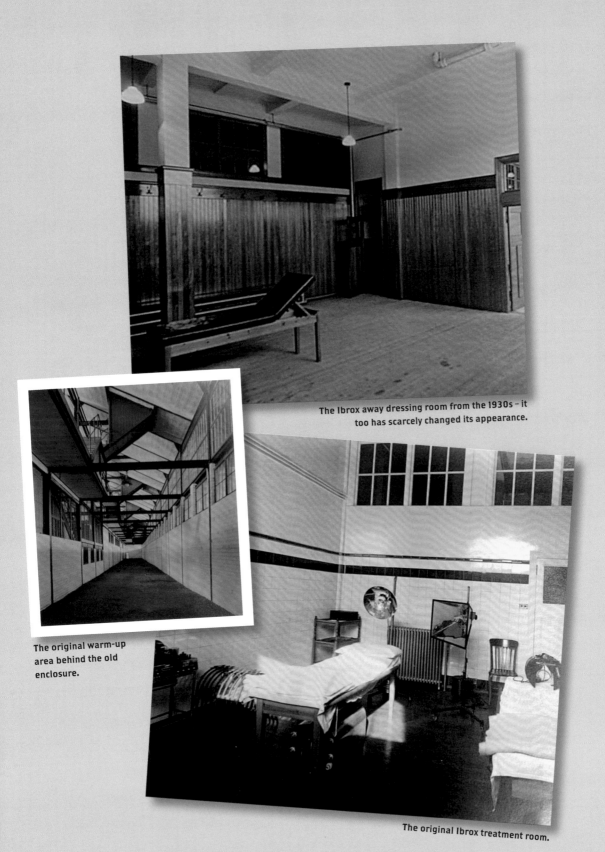

The Ibrox away dressing room from the 1930s – it too has scarcely changed its appearance.

The original warm-up area behind the old enclosure.

The original Ibrox treatment room.

The severe weather caused problems when this shot was taken in the 1950s.

This letter, which was recently unearthed after nearly 50 years, reveals how Walter Smith was once barred from attending Ibrox by one of his legendary predecessors, Scot Symon!

Symon wrote to Smith's father Jack in 1962 turning down a request for his 14-year-old son, who had broken a leg playing football, to sit on the track around the pitch for a home fixture.

Smith had forgotten all about the remarkable correspondence until his sister came across it in their family home in Carmyle in 2010.

FOUNDED 1873

TELEPHONE
IBROX 0158

J. ROGERS SIMPSON, C.A.
SECRETARY

TELEGRAMS
IBROX PARK
GLASGOW

J. S. SYMON
MANAGER

THE RANGERS FOOTBALL CLUB LTD
REGISTERED OFFICE
IBROX STADIUM · GLASGOW · S·W·1

28th. August 1962.

Dear Mr. Smith,

      I regret that I cannot grant permission to your boy to sit on the track. Such a position would be frowned on by the Police, and at the same time expose him to the risk of being struck by the ball.

      Trusting you appreciate our position.

      Please extend to your son our sincere sympathy in his misfortune, and our hopes that he will make a speedy recovery.

      Yours sincerely

Manager.

Mr. W. Smith,
7, Bank Road,
Carmyle,
Glasgow, E.2.

An aerial shot of the stadium from the 1960s.

The Berne Bear.

Carrara Marble Head.

Twisted metal railings on Stairway 13 reveal the full horror of the Ibrox disaster.

Police officers and volunteers try to come to terms with the carnage.

St Andrews Ambulancemen Ian Holmes, Robert Burns and Tom Donaldson were on duty that fateful day.

The Ibrox disaster on January 2, 1971 represents the darkest day in Rangers' history. At the end of the traditional New Year derby, which had finished 1–1, a terrible crush developed on Stairway 13 and claimed the lives of 66 supporters. Their names – along with those from the 1902 and 1961 tragedies – are inscribed on plaques on a statue of John Greig at the corner of the Bill Struth Main Stand and Copland Stand.

These superb aerial shots illustrate how the stadium was modernised to become a 5-star venue.

Richard Gough's medal collection.

Steaua Vase.

Sporting Lisbon Ball.

Sparta Vase.

The façade of Ibrox is one of the most recognised in world football.

The front entrance of Ibrox has changed little in decades.

The foyer at Ibrox is a mixture of marble and solid wood.

The luxurious Members' Club at Ibrox is the ultimate in hospitality.

A shot of the famous marble staircase off the main foyer.

The Ibrox Suite offers a great vista of the stadium.

The Loving Cup was gifted to Rangers by Stoke City chairman St Francis Joseph in 1937 after they took part in a match to raise money in the wake of the Holditch Colliery disaster. Twenty-two cups were cast and given to each English First Division club to commemorate the coronation of King George VI. Sir Francis requested that Rangers toast the Monarch on the first Ibrox game of every new year – something they still do to this day.

The most recent major structural change to Ibrox came in 1991 when a third tier – known as the Club Deck – was added to the Main Stand. It was a fantastic piece of engineering which added to the ambiance of the stadium.

A special marquee was set up on the pitch in 1999 to host a Centenary Ibrox dinner.

The stadium also regularly hosts the Annual General Meeting. This shot is from 2009.

Ibrox is a shrine in so many ways for supporters and the stadium
sadly became one in a literal sense in March 1995 following
the tragic death of Davie Cooper at the age of 39 from a brain
haemorrhage. Cooper played with Rangers from 1977 to 1989 and
his dazzling skills are still revered by many.

This panoramic shot shows the fans' display ahead of the Champions League clash with Inter Milan in 2005. Rangers drew the match 1–1 to qualify for the last 16.

A packed Ibrox on matchday.

Rangers received a special trophy for winning 50 League Championships.

Chapter 8
Old Firm

John Greig and Billy McNeill, 1973, Scottish Cup Final

Derek Johnstone famously scores the winner in the 1970/71 League Cup Final.

ARGUMENTS often rage about the greatest club derby in world football. The citizens of Athens, Belgrade and Buenos Aires may have compelling evidence, but for many there is one fixture that edges them all in terms of rivalry and passion, drama and excitement, and skill and controversy – it's the Old Firm.

RANGERS FOOTBALL CLUB
FINE FARE LEAGUE

CLUB
SPONSORS
C. R. SMITH

RANGERS v.
CELTIC

(Match sponsored by: SUNBLEST BAKERIES LTD.)

IBROX STADIUM, GLASGOW
SATURDAY 22nd MARCH, 1986
KICK-OFF 3.00 p.m.

£4·00

R. C. OGILVIE, Secretary

COPLAND ROAD STAND YELLOW SECTION

REAR
ENTER BY TURNSTILES
1–4 and 15–18

Row	Seat No.
10	26

THIS PORTION TO BE RETAINED BY THE HOLDER

For over 120 years the two heavyweights of Scottish football have gone head to head to produce the most explosive, important and eye-catching occasions ever witnessed in the Scottish game, and it has been lapped up by millions around the globe on television.

Rangers and Celtic are the box-office attractions of the game. Indeed it was for that very reason that the phrase 'Old Firm' was coined at the turn of the 19th century when cynics viewed the two clubs as commercial partners rather than bitter foes.

Of course the rivalry between the two clubs on the field has been fierce since the early 1900s, as they quickly became the biggest clubs in the land. They have won the lion's share of the major honours with Rangers celebrating 114 domestic honours to Celtic's 92.

However, this is exacerbated by their massive supports who largely come from distinct backgrounds – Rangers: Scottish Protestant, Celtic: Irish Roman Catholic. The religious divide gives the fixture a dimension that few other inter-city rivalries have, but the hatred and bitterness it has engendered is undoubtedly unwanted in modern society.

The successes of Rangers and Celtic effectively tell the story of Scottish football because there have only been fleeting periods when one or other has not dominated, like in the 1950s and parts of the early 1960s when Hibs, Hearts, Dundee and Kilmarnock came to the fore, and then in the early 1980s when Aberdeen and Dundee United were kings.

Both clubs can boast nine successive championship successes; Celtic's run coming between 1965/66 and 1973/74 and Rangers achieving the wonderful sequence during the Graeme Souness and Walter Smith eras from 1988/89 to 1996/97.

Equally the attendance records in Scottish football were set when either or both sides were involved. A crowd of 118,567 watched Rangers beat Celtic 2–1 at Ibrox on January 1, 1939 and it remains a British record for a league match that will surely never be surpassed.

In the early days around a dozen players moved between the two sides or played for both sides without causing too much of a fuss. However, in the modern era such acts have been seen as treacherous.

Alfie Conn was part of the Rangers side that famously won the European Cup Winners' Cup in 1972 and scored in the Scottish Cup Final against Celtic the following year. However, he signed for Celtic in 1977 and won a League and Cup Double. Some have never forgiven him.

In the same vein, Celtic supporters still bear a huge grudge against Maurice Johnston. He had been a hero of theirs and was due to return in the summer of 1989 when he sensationally signed for Rangers, and he proceeded to rub salt into deep wounds by regularly scoring against the Parkhead club.

Kenny Miller managed to cross the divide twice having signed for Rangers in 2000, joined Celtic in 2006 and then returned to Rangers via Derby County in 2008. Steven Pressley and Mark Brown are two other players who started with Rangers and subsequently joined Celtic.

Infamously the two sets of fans rioted at the Scottish Cup Finals of 1909 and 1980. Conversely, Rangers formed a guard of honour and applauded Celtic onto the field before a Cup tie in 1964, as Celtic had enjoyed a good result in Europe a few days before defeating Slovan Bratislava 1–0 in Czechoslovakia.

There have been resounding victories for either side, hat-trick heroes most recently in the shape of Ally McCoist for Rangers in 1984, and Harry Hood for Celtic in 1971, and the two sides have drawn 4–4 on two occasions. In essence, it's the fixture that has had it all.

Willie Waddell flies down the wing in an Old Firm
clash at Ibrox from 1953.

**The 1909 Scottish Cup Final between Rangers and Celtic was abandoned and the trophy was withheld when both sets
of fans rioted, fought with police and set fire to anything that would burn. The fans were furious with the authorities
rather than each other because it had been suggested extra time would be played rather than a replay.**

Fearsome striker Jimmy Smith wheels away after another derby goal in the 1930s.

Sandy Archibald wins an aerial battle in the 1928 Scottish Cup final. He scored twice in a 4–0 win.

Rangers keeper Bobby Brown clutches the ball safely. Neil Mochan looks for any mistakes as Willie Woodburn looks on.

Legendary captains Davie Meiklejohn and Jimmy McStay shake hands
ahead of another crucial derby match.

Rangers stalwart and great captain Jimmy Simpson clears from Johnny Crum.
Jimmy's son Ronnie went on to play for Celtic in the late 1960s.

John Greig and Billy McNeill with referee Tom Wharton ahead of the 1966 Scottish Cup Final.
It finished goal-less and Rangers won the replay 1–0 thanks to Kai Johansen.

Tommy McLean, flanked by Tom Forsyth and Alex MacDonald, prepares to meet the truest blue
of them all, Her Majesty Queen Elizabeth, ahead of the Glasgow Select v English League match at
Hampden in May 1977, to celebrate the Silver Jubilee.

Mo Johnston takes aim at Parkhead with a lob shot on November 25, 1990.

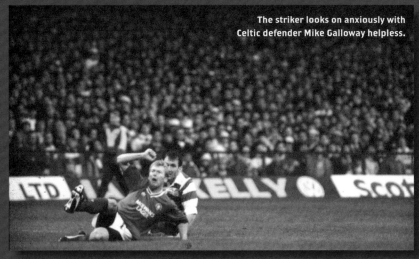

The striker looks on anxiously with Celtic defender Mike Galloway helpless.

Johnston celebrates his goal and Rangers went on to win 2–1.

Alfie Conn in action in the 1973 Scottish Cup Final – in which he scored – with George Connelly in close attendance.

Kenny Miller has the distinction of scoring in Old Firm league matches for both Celtic and Rangers.

Not many players have crossed the Old Firm divide in recent times but the three most high-profile characters are Alfie Conn, Mo Johnston and Kenny Miller. Conn is etched into Rangers' folklore as part of the team that won the Cup Winners' Cup in 1972, but joined Celtic from Tottenham in 1977 and won the Double. Johnston had been a massive hero of the Celtic fans and was due to go back in 1989 from Nantes when Graeme Souness shocked the world and pinched him from under their noses. Miller has crossed the divide twice, having played for Rangers between 2000 and 2001 and 2008 and 2011, and featured for Celtic in the 2006/07 season.

Robert Fleck celebrates a crucial goal in the New Year derby of 1987.

Ally McCoist and Mick McCarthy took their rivalry into paintballing in 1989.

Gordon Marshall's face is a picture as Ally McCoist heads the only goal of the League Cup quarter-final on September 19, 1995.

Paul Gascoigne celebrates a fantastic breakaway goal to give Rangers a 2–0 win over Celtic at Ibrox on September 28, 1996. Rangers won all four league meetings with Celtic that season to clinch Nine in a Row.

Ally McCoist shows
what it means to score
against Celtic as he puts
Rangers ahead in the
1996 Scottish Cup semi-
final which Rangers
won 2–1. In all he scored
27 derby goals.

The fans go wild after Charlie Adam sealed a 2–0 win in May 2007.

Ally McCoist in his Old Firm debut as boss on September 18, 2011. It was a day to remember as Rangers won 4–2.

Ugo Ehiogu celebrates his winner on March 11, 2007.

Davie Weir battles with Celtic striker Georgios Samaras.

Chapter 9
Managers

Sir David Murray and former managers

THE SUN was streaming through the windows of the Blue Room at Ibrox which was packed with pressmen on 22 February, 2011 as Ally McCoist walked in to be announced as only the 13th man to become manager of Rangers.

Bill Struth with captain George Young in the famous Ibrox Manager's Office.

Little did he know then that apart from attempting to shine as a coach, he would became a statesman and a symbolic leader of a club whose very existence was threatened a year later in a gruelling administration process.

It was in the summer of 2011 that the club's greatest goal-scorer assumed the mantle from Walter Smith, who had just completed an astonishing second spell at the club in which he delivered three successive SPL titles, among eight major honours, and an appearance in the 2008 UEFA Cup Final.

For many Smith is Rangers' greatest manager. He had ascended to the manager's chair in a similar fashion to McCoist by working as assistant to Graeme Souness for nearly five years between 1986 and 1991.

He undoubtedly had a fantastic base to work from after Souness revolutionised the game in general by increasing wages and luring top players from England like Terry Butcher, Chris Woods, Graham Roberts, Ray Wilkins, Trevor Steven, Gary Stevens and Mark Hateley.

With a sometimes seat-of-the pants, often incendiary approach, Souness delivered the first title in nine years for Rangers in 1987 and triumphed again in 1989 and 1990 while also delivering the League Cup on four occasions.

He was lured to Liverpool in April 1991 and Smith took over and

It is a fact that Bill Struth is Rangers' most successful manager, with a fabulous haul of 18 League Championships, 10 Scottish Cups and two League Cups, but his tenure lasted an incredible 34 years from 1920 through to 1954.

Struth was only the club's second manager. William Wilton was the first when he was appointed in 1899, but he had already been at the club for 16 years working as secretary for the reserve team and then match secretary to the first team.

by Struth, who had worked with him as the club's trainer.

Struth perpetuated the philosophies and standards of Wilton, ruling with an iron rod at times, as Rangers dominated like never before between the wars.

Former Rangers player Scot Symon was Struth's successor in 1954 and built a new team that would dominate the early 1960s— in particular with swaggering stars like Jim Baxter, Willie Henderson and Davie Wilson and terrific competitors like

Ally McCoist relishes his job.

A bust of the legendary Struth.

Walter Smith – the greatest?

promptly led Rangers to the next seven league titles, equalling Celtic's record of Nine in a Row.

The supporters gorged on the successes of the time as the Scottish Cup and League Cup were claimed three times each and players such as Brian Laudrup and Paul Gascoigne joined the club.

His skills as an administrator and organiser were what the club valued and once he became manager it was Wilton who set the code of discipline for the players which still endures today.

He won seven championships and the Scottish Cup as manager but tragically died in a boating accident in 1920 and was replaced

Bobby Shearer, Ronnie McKinnon and John Greig.

Symon was sacked in 1967 when Rangers were actually top of the league and was replaced by Davie White, whose two-year spell was unsuccessful.

A fantastic club servant, Willie Waddell returned to stabilise the club and he delivered the ultimate dream of winning the European Cup Winners' Cup in 1972. He became general manager and handed the reins over to Jock Wallace who delivered two Trebles in 1976 and 1978.

Greig moved from the dressing room to the manager's office in the summer of 1978 but it was a tough period for the former captain who won two Scottish Cups and two League Cups, but outwith his first season he failed to really challenge for the title.

He resigned in the autumn of 1983 and Wallace returned but only had fleeting success by winning the League Cup twice. He was fired in April 1986 to make way for the dramatic appointment of Souness.

Rangers' first foreign manager, Dick Advocaat, replaced Walter Smith in the summer of 1998 and brought in a multi-national force to replace the Nine in a Row stalwarts. Success was immediate as Rangers won the Treble in his first season.

Advocaat coasted to a League and Cup Double the following season, but things started to unravel in the 2000/01 season and in December of 2001 he handed over the reins to Alex McLeish, who had proved his managerial worth at Motherwell and Hibernian.

With a heavily restricted budget, McLeish coaxed a Cup Double out of the players in 2001/02. He then secured an astonishing clean sweep of the honours the following season, with the title being decided on the final day by virtue of goal difference from Celtic.

A host of top stars left who McLeish was unable to properly replace. However, he delivered the championship again in 2005 on another remarkable final day known as 'Helicopter Sunday'.

Celtic, one point ahead, were expected to win at Motherwell while Rangers faced Hibs at Easter Road. Celtic lost 2-1 and Rangers defeated Hibs 1-0 so a helicopter carrying the SPL trophy changed its flight path to Edinburgh.

In 2006 Rangers took the universally approved step of appointing Frenchman Paul Le Guen, who had delivered three successive Ligue 1 titles with Lyon, in France, and reached the latter stages of the Champions League.

It simply did not work. After just 31 matches, Le Guen left, with Rangers effectively out of the title race and embarrassingly eliminated at home in the League Cup by a lower league side for the first time, in the shape of St Johnstone.

There was only one man to call and that was Smith, who undoubtedly mentored McCoist for the challenges ahead.

David Murray formally announces the return of Smith in January 2007.

McCoist shows his colours.

Rangers' first manager William Wilton was a hugely influential figure in the early years of the Light Blues. He had been a key man in the late 1800s before becoming manager in 1899, and set the standards for the club which remain in force today.

Bill Struth's record of achievements was extraordinary. He won the League
Championship 18 times, including a dazzling spell of 14 in 19 years before the war.
Those titles included a run of Five in a Row between 1926/27 and 1930/31,
a standard unsurpassed at the club until the 1990s. Not only was he to bring the
first Cup and League Double to the club in 1927/28, he was still at the helm when
they completed the first League, Cup and League Cup Treble in 1948/49.

The legendary manager at his desk in the Ibrox Manager's Office, which has scarcely changed in appearance since he was the occupant.

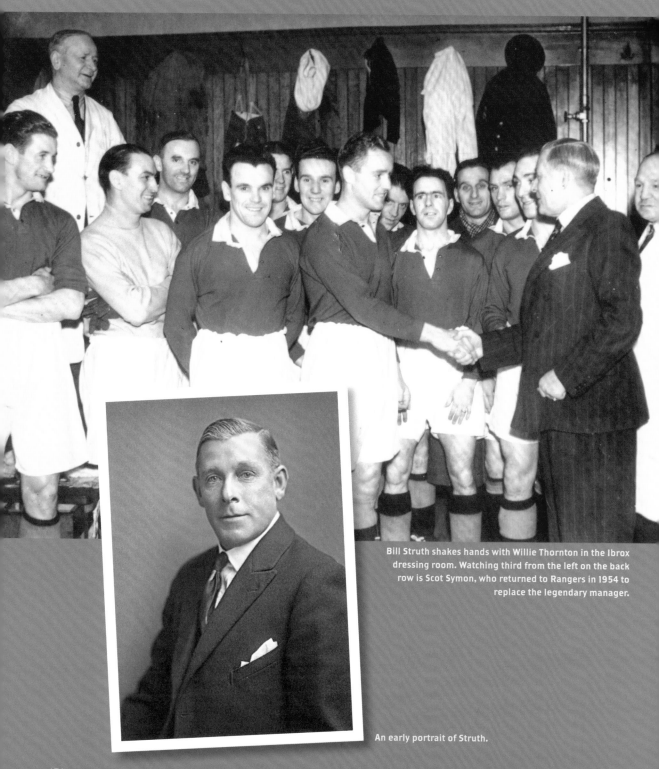

Bill Struth shakes hands with Willie Thornton in the Ibrox dressing room. Watching third from the left on the back row is Scot Symon, who returned to Rangers in 1954 to replace the legendary manager.

An early portrait of Struth.

Scot Symon led Rangers to 15 major honours – including the Treble in
1963/64 – and two European Cup Winners' Cup Finals, 1961 and 1967.

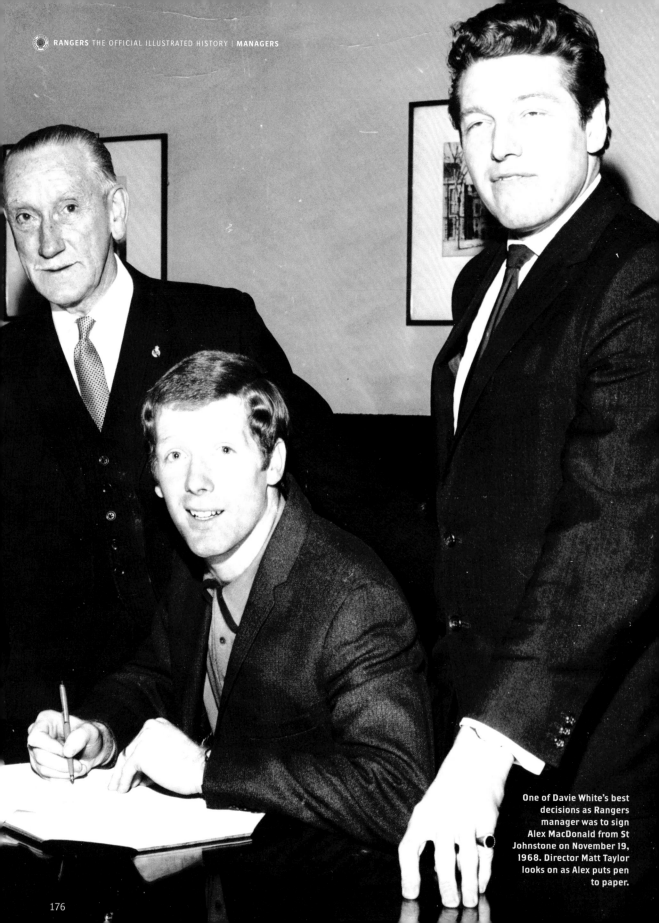

One of Davie White's best decisions as Rangers manager was to sign Alex MacDonald from St Johnstone on November 19, 1968. Director Matt Taylor looks on as Alex puts pen to paper.

Willie Waddell was the Rangers manager who delivered European glory
with the Cup Winners' Cup triumph in 1972, but he was also a hugely
influential figure in his role as General Manager, most notably for
restructuring Ibrox as a modern stadium.

Jock Wallace was a tough character, but got the best
out of his players in two spells as Rangers boss.

Wallace shows his colours as Rangers win the title at Easter Road in 1975.

The silver was gleaming in 1976 when Jock Wallace led Rangers to the Treble of League, Scottish Cup and League Cup and the Light Blues also won the Premier Reserve League and the Glasgow Cup into the bargain.

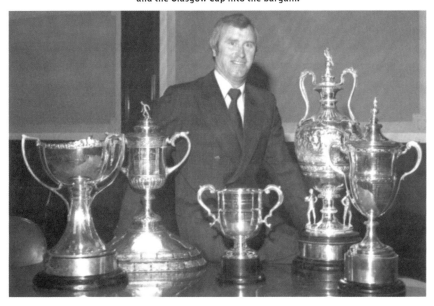

Jock Wallace visited the Ibrox Trophy Room with his wife Daphne in his later years.

Wallace joined Walter Smith to celebrate the title win of 1994.

The League Cup was sponsored in the 1980s by Skol who produced their own trophy to supplement the original, and Wallace was successful twice in the same year, winning in March 1984 and then in November 1984.

Ian Durrant and Ally McCoist with Jock in the Ibrox dugout.

John Greig went straight from the dressing room to the manager's office in 1978 and nearly won the Treble in his first season. He won the Scottish Cup and League Cup twice as Ibrox boss.

Greig rallies his troops as extra time looms in the epic 1979 Scottish Cup Final which needed a second replay before Rangers triumphed over Hibs, winning 3–2.

Greig puts Rangers through their paces at the old Albion training ground.

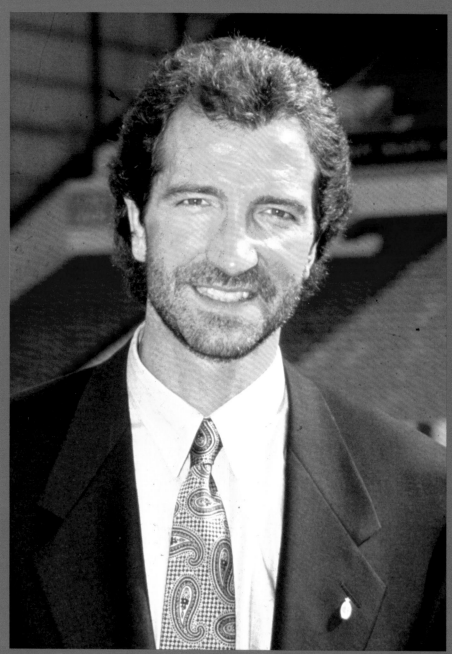

The appointment of Graeme Souness as player–manager in 1986 by David Holmes
was a master-stroke. He re-awoke Rangers and revolutionised the Scottish game,
winning three League titles and four League Cups in five years.

Souness proudly shows off the silverware
after Rangers' title triumph in 1990.

Walter Smith was Souness's trusty lieutenant.

Graeme Souness

Injuries limited the playing appearances of Souness but in his pomp he was a joy to behold in the Rangers midfield.

April 1991 was a momentous period as Souness sensationally announced he was leaving Rangers for Liverpool. Chairman David Murray could not hide his disappointment, but he was all smiles after making Walter Smith the new boss.

Walter Smith brought incredible success in his second spell as manager.

Walter Smith

Walter enjoys life in the old Ibrox dugout during the trophy-laden 1990s.

Rangers regularly used the Italian training camp of
Il Ciocco to prepare for the challenges ahead.

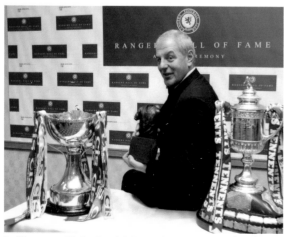

Smith poses with the Scottish Cup and SPL trophy and (right)
stands proudly in the Ibrox Trophy Room.

Smith officially waved his farewells to the Ibrox fans on May 10, 2011.

Ally McCoist and Walter Smith celebrate the 2011 title triumph.

David Murray welcomes Smith back to Rangers in 2007.

Dick Advocaat became Rangers' first foreign manager in 1998.

**The Dutchman is hoisted into the air after Rangers clinched the Double in
2000 to follow the Treble he achieved in his first season in charge.**

Advocaat admires some special footwear
presented to him in Holland.

The 'Little General' celebrates the 1999
SPL title with assistant Bert van Lingen.

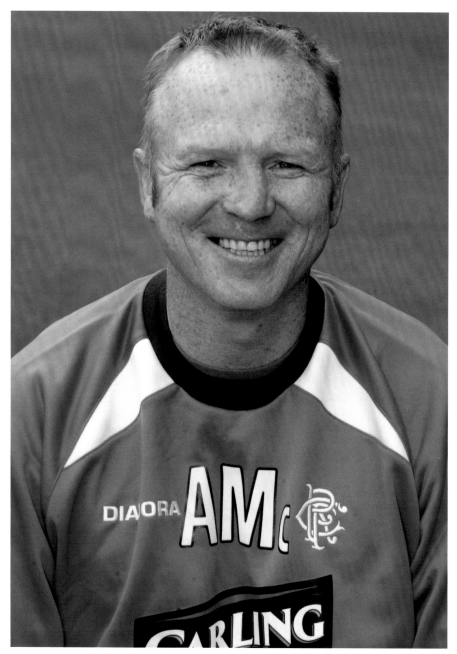

Alex McLeish was Rangers boss from December 2001 to May 2006.

McLeish is unveiled as boss, with Dick Advocaat becoming Director of Football.

Alex takes the acclaim of the Rangers fans.

McLeish proudly displays the Treble he won in 2003.

The appointment of Frenchman Paul Le Guen in 2006 was universally approved of after his successes with Lyon, but the move did not work out and he left the club in January 2007.

It was a proud moment for Ally McCoist when he was announced as Walter Smith's successor in February 2011 having been groomed and mentored by Smith over the previous four years.

Ally McCoist with Ian Durrant at his first match in charge against German lower league side Sportfreunde Lotte on July 7, 2011.

Chapter 10
Heroes and legends

Brian Laudrup, Scotland's Player of the Year 1995

THE word 'legend' is inappropriately applied in football more than any other sport when mediocre players are often elevated to a status that they do not deserve. However, Rangers can boast a host of men who are more than worthy of the accolade.

Paul Gascoigne signs for Rangers in the summer of 1995.

Debates will always rage about who were the greatest players to pull on a blue jersey and there are differing reasons for putting certain individuals on a pedestal – sheer talent, brilliant leadership, success on the field and longevity.

For these compelling reasons the official Rangers Hall of Fame was set up in 1999 on the back of an event which celebrated the Greatest Rangers XI following a poll among supporters.

Unsurprisingly, the vote was loaded towards the most recent stars and produced a side which read: Andy Goram, Sandy Jardine, Richard Gough, Terry Butcher, John Greig, Brian Laudrup, Paul Gascoigne, Jim Baxter, Davie Cooper, Ally McCoist, Mark Hateley.

There is no disputing the talent, impact and glory that all of these players had during their playing careers at Ibrox but supporters of an older vintage could offer a side like this: Jerry Dawson, George Young, Davie Meiklejohn, Willie Woodburn, Eric Caldow, Willie Waddell, Ian McColl, Tommy Muirhead, Alan Morton, Bob McPhail and Willie Thornton.

Indeed, it is completely feasible to produce two more 'greatest Rangers XIs', such has been the plethora of fantastic players who have made their own mark on the club with their performances and heroics.

Rangers have been blessed with superb captains throughout their history, stretching back to Tom Vallance in the fledgling days of the club, through Muirhead and the incomparable Meiklejohn in the 1920s and 1930s, through to Jock Shaw and Young in the 1940s and 1950s.

Indeed, Young was also captain of the Scottish national team in 48 of 53 appearances, and at a time when teams were selected by committee, he ran the national team arranging training, theatre visits and even booked local transport.

Subsequently John Greig had a similar impact on Rangers. Even if his captaincy was difficult in the early stages when Celtic were dominant, it was a joy to behold in the 1970s when Rangers lifted the European Cup Winners' Cup and won two Trebles.

In more recent times Richard Gough was a fantastic leader in the Nine in a Row years, while Davie Weir defied the march of time with model performances on and off the field under the managership of Walter Smith.

Of course, the fans relate more exuberantly to the entertainers; the men who make things happen or fire the ball into the net. There has been a great tradition of wingers at Rangers, even if this aspect of the game is a dying art in modern times.

Alex Smith was the original superstar, from the turn of the 19th century, with his wing play and his tally of 151 goals in 481 appearances; while Alan Morton – the man nicknamed the 'Wee Blue Devil' – was an equal in terms of box-office appeal in the early Bill Struth years.

Waddell and Thornton had an almost telepathic understanding that produced so many goals for Rangers in the early post-war years, and then the skills of Willie Henderson and Davie Wilson on the flanks of the great Scot Symon side thrilled the Ibrox legions.

Between them was arguably the most talented of them all – Jim Baxter. Those who saw him say Baxter in full flow was like an orchestra conductor. He had beautiful ball skills, an exceptional left foot and the vision and time to make space for others to play in.

Davie Cooper in full fight was undoubtedly a joy to behold. There was scarcely anyone like him again at Rangers until Brian Laudrup arrived and produced displays that were literally jaw-dropping, as he left defenders bemused and bewildered before delivering a killer pass or a vital goal.

In terms of strikers McPhail, Jimmy Smith and Jimmy Fleming were the kings of the pre-war, with an astonishing 730 goals between them.

Derek Johnstone is a member of their 200-goals-plus club, which is all the more remarkable given that he regularly played at centre-half or in midfield.

In recent times, the club's greatest goal-scorer, Ally McCoist, accentuated his hero status with the way he handled the turbulent administration process. Here's hoping there are more legends to emerge in the years ahead.

Tough centre-back Willie Woodburn was
a key man in the Iron Curtain defence.

Electric winger Alex Scot lit up the
late 1950s and early 1960s.

Andy Cunningham.

Willie Thornton.

Bobby Main, Jerry Dawson, Jimmy Simpson and Sandy Archibald.

'The Wee Blue Devil' Alan Morton was
the entertainer in the 1920s and 1930s.

Billy Simpson was a fantastic
Rangers striker in the 1950s

Prolific Ralph Brand scores against Hibs.

Dougie Gray.

Bobby Shearer.

George Young was a colossus for Rangers in more ways than one.

John Greig won three Trebles and was
voted the 'Greatest Ranger' by fans.

Tom Forsyth was the fan's hero in the
1970s for his stout defending.

Many feel Jim Baxter was the most talented star to play for Rangers. He had a fantastic swagger about his play and thrilled the supporters in the early 1960s when the Light Blues dominated the game.

Baxter was pure box office for the
Rangers supporters who idolised him
in much the same way that movie stars
or pop stars were adored.

There has scarcely been a more exciting Rangers player than Davie Cooper, whose mesmerising skills were a joy to behold. Tragically, he died at the age of 39 in 1995 following a brain haemorrhage.

The quality of Derek Johnstone cannot be underestimated as he played superbly well as a striker, a centre-back or in midfield. He burst onto the scene at 16, scoring the winner in the 1970/71 League Cup Final, and scored 210 goals in total.

Class, quality and loyalty all accurately
describe Sandy Jardine, who played 778
games for Rangers including friendlies –
mostly at right-back, during an incredible
career which included two Trebles and the
European Cup Winners' Cup. He was voted
Scottish Football Writers' Player of the Year
in 1975 and then again in 1986 when he
was with Hearts in the twilight of his career.

Ian Durrant and Ian Ferguson were rivals when the latter played with St Mirren but both became heroes at Ibrox during the Nine in a Row era. Durrant was undoubtedly one of the greatest talents in the game, but a terrible knee injury robbed him of the best part of three years. Ferguson is one of only three players who have all nine medals – the others are Richard Gough and Ally McCoist.

Ally McCoist is Rangers' greatest goal-scorer with a tally of 355 which will surely never be surpassed. His partnership with Mark Hateley in the 1990s was one of the best the game has ever seen. McCoist won ten titles, nine League Cups and the Scottish Cup once.

The world sat up and took notice when
Walter Smith pulled off the stunning coup
of signing Brian Laudrup from Fiorentina
in 1994. Laudrup's skills were some of
the greatest ever seen at Ibrox and it was
the Great Dane who scored the goal that
clinched Nine in a Row at Tannadice in 1997.

Few had heard of Jorg Albertz when Walter Smith signed him from Hamburg in 1996, but he became a legendary figure, especially with his shooting power which earned him the nickname 'The Hammer'.

Albertz celebrated with fellow German Stefan Klos after Aberdeen were demolished 4–0 in the 2000 Scottish Cup Final.

The legends from the famous friendly against Moscow Dynamo in 1945 and the heroes from Barcelona 1972
were introduced to the fans when the Russians came to Ibrox on February 13, 1985.

Rangers supporters never tired of watching the
maverick genius that was Gazza in full flow.

Iron Curtain defender Sammy Cox was voted into the Hall of Fame, as was Graeme Souness.

Three great captains together – Richard Gough, Jock Shaw and John Greig.

Ronald de Boer high-fives the fans after scoring at Parkhead.

Walter Smith meets the legendary Bob McPhail, who is second
on the all-time Rangers scoring chart for league goals with 233.
He won nine titles and five Scottish Cups in the amazing 1920s
and 1930s era.

Davie Weir emerged as a great Rangers captain with five years of
great service which took him through his 41st birthday, making
him the oldest to play for the Light Blues.

Chapter 11
Behind the Scenes

Ronald de Boer, pre-season, Germany, 2003

The **LEGENDARY** Bill Shankly once said that 'football is not a matter of life and death – it's more important than that'. It was a typically tongue-in-cheek yet partially serious comment from the man who transformed Liverpool in the 1960s and regularly used clever commentary to make his point.

Of course, games are often ferocious and intense with so much at stake for those involved and those watching, so it is no surprise that players like to unwind when the pressures of the pitch are removed.

Golf was something the players of the 1920s and 1930s turned to, although in the 1980s Graeme Souness was not a big fan and banned his players from hitting the fairways when he was in charge in case they got injured!

Thankfully for the keen golfers, Walter Smith relaxed that rule in his tenure. Indeed, he and

Ally McCoist still have regular battles on the course, with Ian Durrant and Kenny McDowall also involved.

Of course other players have different passions. Peter Lovenkrands, for example, is a basketball fanatic and partly realised his dream when he got to shoot some hoops with the Glasgow Rocks during his days at Ibrox.

Steven Thompson, conversely, is a highly accomplished angler and can also play the guitar to a very high standard.

wear a garish green and white hooped number.

Equally, the Rangers players have had the experience of travelling to some fascinating locations and in recent years the Rangers Media team have been with them to get some fantastic behind-the-scenes shots.

There were hard training sessions in the Tuscan location of Il Ciocco, but the players could relax afterwards. This has been the same at most of the pre-season training camps, with many players

Equally, six years earlier the squad was in Toronto, in Canada, and they were able to visit the CN Tower – the world's largest structure – and also the spectacular Niagara Falls a couple of hours south.

In 2002 the squad was based in leafy New Jersey and had the opportunity to get into the Big Apple for some leisure and recreation time, which most gleefully took advantage of.

Surely the most bizarre travel story must be from 2007 when

Basile Boli and Brian Laudrup get into the Christmas spirit.

Ally McCoist doesn't fancy his hand in a game of cards in Il Ciocco with Mo Johnston just days after the former Celtic star signed.

Invariably, all the players are game for a laugh and there was always a tradition from the late 1980s onwards to dress up for the Christmas Party – and the lads of the late 2000s have followed that for sure!

Wild suits were created for the 2008 party and it was Mo Edu who was the unlucky one who had to

choosing to worship the sun after some intense work on the field.

In Australia in 2010, however, the Rangers stars had the chance to visit the world-famous Bondi Beach just outside Sydney and try to show their skills on a surfboard. Some were more balanced than others ...

Rangers were preparing to face Hapoel Tel Aviv in the UEFA Cup. They arrived at Glasgow Airport to find that Iron Maiden lead singer Bruce Dickinson was flying them to Israel!

Walter Smith and Ally McCoist might have run to the hills but they were thrilled to meet the rock idol.

Alan Morton (above and below) and Jimmy Fleming proved they were in more than ship shape for a transatlantic voyage with Rangers in 1928

'The Wee Blue Devil' was also a keen golfer

South African Johnny Hubbard looks stylish back in 1951.

Tommy Muirhead had many
tasks as Rangers captain but
training Bill Struth's dog was
certainly an unusual one.

Jimmy Millar, Jim Baxter and Ralph Brand relax at a pavement café in Seville before a Cup Winners' Cup clash in 1962.

Willie Henderson and Jim Baxter enjoy a glass of milk as Davie Wilson looks on with Alex Willoughby in the background.

Eric Caldow signed this shot of Jim Baxter, Bobby Shearer and himself heading to the Albion training ground.

Scot Symon greets Tottenham manager Bill Nicholson before the sides met in the Cup Winners' Cup in 1962.

These amazing snapshots were taken by Derek Johnstone ahead of the 1972 European Cup Winners' Cup Final in Barcelona. Alex MacDonald looks like he needs some sunscreen and so does commentator Archie Macpherson (bottom right).

225

Gary Stevens took every opportunity to enjoy his spare time at Rangers' training camp at Il Ciocco.

Boss Graeme Souness certainly worked the players hard at the centre in the Tuscan hills of Italy.

The legendary Sean Connery, Dick Advocaat and John Greig raise a smile as they watch training in Prague in 2002.

Chris Woods looks a little apprehensive as 'stylist' Ian Ferguson prepares to cut his hair.

Gazza and Ally McCoist with Bob Monkhouse at a dinner to celebrate Nine in a Row.

Ian Durrant salutes McCoist's MBE award.

Ally McCoist and
former world boxing
champion Barry
McGuigan received
MBEs on the same
day in 1994.

Arthur Numan takes advantage of the facilities on the beach in Dubai in 2003.

It's a fair cop for Michael Mols after the 2003 Scottish Cup Final.

Paul Gascoigne and John Greig at the Greatest Rangers dinner in 1999.

Paul Gascoigne

The inimitable Gazza was a proud England player but he got into the full Braveheart spirit for this exclusive picture in 1996.

Andy Watson, Alex McLeish and Jan Wouters model Ralph Lauren sunglasses.

Barry Ferguson shows his skills on the cobbles of a Glasgow lane.

Rino Gattuso looking cool.

Lorenzo Amoruso gets in the ring.

MacKonterman!

Fernando Ricksen, Dado Prso and Alex Rae in kilts.

Michael Mols and son Nino.

An exclusive shot of the Rangers dressing room on pre-season in Germany in 2009.

Peter Lovenkrands playing basketball.

Davie Weir and Christan Dailly at the Acropolis in Athens.

Prso and Vignal read all about it in Red Square before facing CSKA Moscow.

Craig Moore at Dubai Creek Golf Club.

Nacho Novo on the Clyde Water Taxi.

Celebrity chef and massive Rangers fan Gordon Ramsay spent a day at
Murray Park when he joined in training and helped prepare food in the kitchen.

Jan Wouters at spectacular Niagara Falls in 2005.

Iron Maiden lead singer Bruce Dickinson flew Rangers to Israel in 2007.

Pedro Mendes catches some shut-eye on pre-season 2009.

Dado Prso admires a shot of John Greig in the Hampden museum.

Lee McCulloch and Mo Edu get ready for the Christmas party.

What a garish bunch! The players en route for festive fun.

Barry Ferguson is slick in sliver while Kyle Lafferty has the purple look.

Chris Burke is ready for combat, it seems, with Kirk Broadfoot.

Allan McGregor has a touch of the Green Lantern going on.

Nacho Novo and Pedro Mendes are cool in gold and white.

Stevie Thompson, Nacho Novo and Barry Ferguson at the CN Tower in Toronto.

Stevie Thompson fishing at Carbeth Fishery.

Kyle Lafferty surfing on Bondi Beach in Australia in July 2010.

Ian Durrant and Kenny McDowall got on their bikes in Germany in July 2011.

Steve Davis riding the waves at
Bondi Beach in Australia 2010.

Ally McCoist met Lower Saxony Prime
Minister David McAllister in 2011.

Although born in Germany, Lower Saxony Prime Minister David McAllister is proud of his Scottish roots and followed his father in supporting Rangers. He met the team at their training camp near Herzlake in 2011.

Rangers have always had a close bond with the services and the 1 Medical Regiment from Munster were special guests at their training camp.

Kenny McDowall, Ally McCoist and Ian Durrant show their support for Mo-vember.

Ally McCoist met troops from 1 Medical Regiment from Munster in July 2011.

Chapter 12
The Fans

One fan shows her feelings

Veteran fan Andy Bain.

Fans show their feelings at Hampden after a protest march in April 2012.

THE passion, commitment and loyalty of the Rangers' supporters was never more apparent than in the turbulent early part of 2012 when the very existence of their beloved club was threatened.

They showed a remarkable spirit of support as they rallied round at the club's time of need to sell out home matches, plunge thousands of pounds into the Rangers Fans Fighting Fund and dug even deeper to purchase a variety of club products to maintain a cash flow.

Despite facing a desperately uncertain future as Rangers tried to deal with the horror of mismanagement and the pain of administration, the supporters displayed great resilience.

However, no-one should really have been surprised because the strength of feeling of Rangers' supporters runs deep and there was no way they were going to meekly surrender.

From the very early days, Rangers have been a huge attraction and now you will find supporters from Azerbaijan to Winnipeg; from Belfast to Wanganui, and Dubai to Katowice. There are even a couple of supporters clubs in the unlikely setting of Dublin.

There are diehards like Gordon Young and Ross Blyth (also vice-president of the Rangers Supporters Assembly) who travel

Veteran Andy Bain, who lost a leg in the Second World War, has seen Rangers in every League Cup final since 1946/47 and has scarcely missed any matches in this period, latterly accompanied by entertainer Andy Cameron.

But these are just some small examples of thousands of Rangers supporters who have given their backing to the team all over the globe at different times.

When football began to boom in the early 1900s, Rangers were at the forefront in terms of crowds.

Old Firm win at Ibrox on January 2, 1939 created a Scottish league record that stands to this day and will surely never be surpassed.

That said, the greatest average attendances at Ibrox are not from the 1930s or the immediate post-war years. Neither are they from the swinging sixties nor the Treble-winning seventies.

It is in the last 15 years that these records have been set when Ibrox has been filled almost to its 51,082 capacity at every home match in the SPL. Season ticket sales are a massive percentage of that, though, whereas in bygone days most fans paid at the gate.

Thousands of fans on the tarmac at Prestwick Airport welcome Rangers back from their 1962 tour of the Soviet Union.

to the ends of the earth to follow their team – whether it is in Sydney, Australia, or deepest Lower Saxony, in Germany, on pre-season tours.

Gordon even made it all the way to Dagestan when Rangers were due to play Anzhi Makhachkala in 2001 when the game was called off for security reasons.

Then, as now, Old Firm games were the big attraction, but 60,000 watched Rangers draw with Alloa in the Cup in 1921 and then 55,000 watched the replay.

The first 100,000-plus crowd was created when Rangers beat Celtic 4–0 in the 1928 Scottish Cup final when 118,115 saw it happen. The 118,730 that watched a 2–1 home

The phrase 'loyal and true' has never been more applicable than to the Rangers supporters; there are 600 registered supporters clubs throughout the UK, a well-organised North American Rangers Supporters Association and a similar set-up Down Under with the Oceanic Rangers Supporters Association.

They remain the stakeholders and the beating heart of Rangers Football Club.

Skipper John Greig is mobbed by exuberant fans after the 1972 European Cup Winners' Cup Final.

Thousands gather outside the St Enoch's Hotel in the 1960s.

Supporters on matchday outside Ibrox in the early 1960s.

John Greig is presented with an award by this happy bunch of fans.

These patriotic youngsters met Ronald de Boer, Mike Arteta and Stephen Hughes in New York in 2003.

One young fan shows his colours at the 2003 title-clincher.

Ally McCoist was thrilled to meet AC/DC rocker Malcolm Young, who collected a special shirt for his brother Angus.

Lifelong fan Colin Montgomerie was presented with this special strip by John Greig to celebrate his eight European Order of Merit victories.

Model Nell McAndrew helped launch the kit for 2002/03 and it proved to be
a lucky omen as Rangers won the Treble.

Fans parade with the SPL and League Cup trophies at the start of the 2011/12 season.

The fans rejoice with Lee Wallace after his goal against Celtic in 2011.

Ibrox awash with colour.

Skipper Davie Weir is mobbed after winning the League Cup in 2011.

Supporters celebrate the 2009 SPL title in some style.

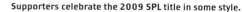

The loyal Rangers supporters back their team in Valencia in the Champions League in 2011.

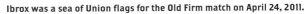

Ibrox was a sea of Union flags for the Old Firm match on April 24, 2011.

The Rangers fans ahead of the Champions League meeting with Manchester United in 2010.

Sasa Papac mobbed by fans at Kilmarnock after the 2011 League triumph.

The victorious players take a bow at Rugby Park after winning Three in a Row in 2011.

Ally McCoist's leadership in the administration period is saluted by supporters.

The Rangers supporters have been incredible since life began in Division Three and they set a world record attendance of 49,118 for a fourth tier game when Rangers faced East Stirlingshire in their opening home fixture on August 18, 2012.

The rush to buy season tickets for the 2012/13 season was amazing with fans queuing for hours producing over 36,000 sales.

Spanish star Fran Sandaza joined the supporters at the Ticket Centre as they backed the club with season ticket sales.